Word Alive

Bible teaching at the cutting edge

Word
Alive

Editor: David Porter

Lindsay Brown
Roy Clements
Dick Dowsett
Stephen Gaukroger
Philip Hacking
David Jackman
Jonathan Lamb
Nigel Lee
Dick Lucas
Hugh Palmer

Inter-Varsity Press

INTER-VARSITY PRESS
38 De Montfort Street, Leicester LE1 7GP, England

Unless otherwise stated, Scripture quotations in this publication are from the Holy Bible, New International Version. Copyright © 1973, 1978, 1984 International Bible Society. Published in Great Britain by Hodder and Stoughton Ltd.

First published 1994

British Library Cataloguing in Publication Data
A catalogue record for this book is available from the British Library.

ISBN 0–85110–996–9

Set in Palatino

Typeset in Great Britain by Parker Typesetting Service, Leicester
Printed in Great Britain by Cox & Wyman Ltd, Reading

Inter-Varsity Press is the book-publishing division of the Universities and Colleges Christian Fellowship (formerly the Inter-Varsity Fellowship), a student movement linking Christian Unions in universities and colleges throughout the United Kingdom and the Republic of Ireland, and a member movement of the International Fellowship of Evangelical Students. For information about local and national activities write to UCCF, 38 De Montfort Street, Leicester LE1 7GP.

Contents

Preface

Word Alive 1993 was a great event! One prominent church leader even called it 'epoch-making'!

Three evangelical Christian agencies – Keswick Convention, Proclamation Trust and the Universities and Colleges Christian Fellowship – collaborated with Spring Harvest to plan a major holiday conference at Pwllheli in North Wales. It attracted over 5,000 attenders.

In many ways it was very similar to the Spring Harvest weeks that have drawn hundreds of thousands of Christians during the Easter period in recent years. The programme blended contemporary praise and worship with a demanding schedule of in-depth teaching in both small and large groups. But Word Alive did have a distinctive feel to it.

First, it put a very special emphasis on the exposition of the Bible.

Second, it aimed to meet the needs of the 1,000 Christian students who came. It was the largest such gathering ever in the UK, compelling evidence of the immense strength of Christian Unions in the tertiary education institutions of Britain today.

Third, it brought together a wider spectrum of evangelicals than probably any other event of recent years. The divisions between the Anglican and Free Churches, and between charismatic and non-charismatic believers, have seriously weakened evangelicalism. Word Alive went at least some way towards the bridging of those rifts.

I want to pay tribute to a number of people who played a key role in the success of Word Alive. The event could never have got beyond the drawing board if it had not enjoyed the personal support of Robin Wells (former General Secretary of UCCF), Philip Hacking (Chairman of the Keswick Convention Committee) and David Jackman (representing Proclamation Trust). The enthusiasm of Clive Calver, Stephen

Gaukroger and Alan Johnson from Spring Harvest has been absolutely indispensable too. More recently Elaine Duncan, Bob Dawson and Bob Horn (all of UCCF), David Gray (of Keswick) and Jonathan Juckes (of Proclamation Trust) have played a very valuable part. And a debt of gratitude is owed to Ian Macdowell (formerly of UCCF, now of Spring Harvest) whose administrative skill and energy were of immense importance. There is one contribution, however, that ought not to be forgotten. In October 1991 a small group of Christian leaders and their partners met at Fairmile Court in Surrey for a time of mutual fellowship, discussion and prayer. It was there that my own wife, Jane, first came up with the idea of Word Alive. It quickly germinated among the group and thus the vision was born.

It has long been my belief that only when we place our shared commitment to the authority of the Bible at the centre will evangelical Christians experience the unity for which they long. I know that belief is shared by all those who joined hands to make Word Alive 1993 possible and the success of the event amply confirmed our confidence in this respect. I believe a new platform for co-operation between evangelical Christians was established there with enormous potential for the future. But it was only a beginning. Time will tell whether it was the beginning of a new 'epoch' or just a 'flash in the pan'. My prayer is that it will prove to be the former. Inter-Varsity Press is producing this book of Word Alive 1993 addresses in that hope also. If you find these pages exciting, share them with others. Better still, plan to join us at Word Alive in the future!

Roy Clements
Chairman of the Organizing Committee

Editor's introduction

The material that follows represents a substantial amount of the ministry from the first Spring Harvest Word Alive week.

It is important to bear in mind that this book is the edited transcript of a spoken occasion. Though a great deal of editorial work and checking have taken place, the text remains a transcript rather than the manuscript that the speakers would have written had they been intending book or journal publication. Also, they have had limited opportunity to review the edited text. My aim in editing has been to reflect the atmosphere of the event, to convey the speaking style of the various speakers, and to include all the content of the addresses while judiciously abridging them as book publication demands. One consequence of this is that you may well want to make use of the original tapes. Details of how to purchase them are provided at the end of the book.

Every reference to a Bible quotation has been included, though some have remained as references, where in the original addresses they were read out in full; others have been shortened. You will get the most out of this book, therefore, if you read it with a Bible at your side, looking up all the references. Where no version is cited, quotations are from the NIV. Where a speaker is paraphrasing, this is indicated by '*cf.*' before the reference, unless it is quite clear from the context that a paraphrase or imaginative reconstruction of dialogue is involved. Greek transliterations follow W. E. Vine's *Expository Dictionary of New Testament Words*.

I would like to thank the small army of typists who transcribed the original tapes, and the editorial staff of IVP; also to acknowledge a major reference source I have used for checking missionary and global facts and figures – Patrick Johnstone's unfailingly reliable *Operation World* (OM Publishing, 5th edition 1993). And I would like to thank Spring

Word Alive

Harvest Word Alive and IVP for the opportunity to work on this material. I once described my enjoyable task of editing the annual Keswick Convention volume as 'like being let loose in a theological chocolate factory'. To have that experience twice in one year is indeed a privilege and a pleasure.

David Porter

The sins of half-heartedness

Studies in Malachi

by Roy Clements

I

Doubt

Malachi 1:1–5

We knocked on the door and went in. The mother burst into tears almost immediately, and pointed to the little cot in the corner. We knew already that it was her first baby, for whom she and her husband had been praying for many months. The child had been born handicapped. Between sobs, the mother blurted out the question: 'Does God care?'

It is the question we always ask when any kind of tragedy strikes. It was the question that Jews had been asking for a couple of centuries, long before Malachi had arrived on the scene. They had had so long to grieve that now they no longer expressed their doubt about God's care through tears, but with a sarcastic curl of the lips and a wearied shrug of the shoulders.

'"I have loved you," says the LORD. "But you ask, 'How have you loved us?'"'(Mal. 1:2).

Almost everybody who has ever tried their hand at open-air preaching has encountered the heckler; the person who shouts from the audience in an attempt to throw you off your stroke or embarrass you. Martin Luther probably delivered the best response to such an interruption. A trouble-maker demanded loudly, 'Well, what was God doing before he made the world then?' Luther, quoting his theological mentor Augustine, is reputed to have replied: 'Making hell for people who ask stupid questions like that!'

If you have ever faced that kind of hostile questioning, you will have plenty of sympathy for Malachi, for it seems that there were plenty of hecklers disturbing his attempt at public speaking too. Every time he makes a statement throughout the course of these four chapters, some sarcastic or dismissive retort is thrown back at him from his audience. Here is the first example. 'I have loved you,' says the Lord. 'But you ask, "How? You don't expect us to believe that!"'

Another example: 'You have despised God's name,' says Malachi.

'Prove it!' shouts back the wise-cracker (*cf.* 1:6).

Again in chapter 2: 'You have wearied the Lord,' he says.

'Pull the other leg, Malachi,' comes the riposte (*cf.* 2:17).

'You are robbing God,' he asserts.

'Stuff and nonsense,' they reply (*cf.* 3:8).

Some commentators regard this heckling dialogue merely as a literary device to express the unresponsiveness of Malachi's contemporaries. But to me it sounds far more like authentic, live reporting.

Imagine, then, Malachi preaching his open-air sermon in the Jerusalem market place. But his hearers are giving him a rough ride. It is quite clear that the Jews to whom he is speaking do not feel they deserve his prophetic rebukes and comment. 'What right has this fellow to criticize us?' they say. 'We are not irreligious – why, if anyone deserves to be put into the dock, it is God. Considering all we have done for him, he has done very little for us. He just does not care.' And superficially perhaps they had grounds for their indignation.

For Malachi's hearers are not faithless apostates. There *had* been a time a few centuries earlier when prophets like Elijah, Isaiah and Jeremiah had had very good grounds for their pulpit invective. For Baal worship was corrupting the people then.

But now all that was past history. These Jews to whom Malachi speaks are not like that any more. God punished the Jews for all their previous idolatry. He sent them into Babylonian exile for seventy years, and that chastening experience has, to a considerable extent, had the desired effect. They have learned the folly of their idolatrous ways, they have come to appreciate their national heritage and want to preserve it. Indeed, so committed are they to their Jewish culture and their Jewish religion now that this particular group of Jews had actually sacrificed what for many of them would have been quite a comfortable and prosperous existence in Babylon. They had returned to Judah to rebuild the temple in Jerusalem and to reoccupy the city and reconstruct its ruined walls. You can read the whole story in the books of Ezra and Nehemiah.

Of course, it did not all happen in a few days. Malachi is preaching his sermon some ninety or hundred years after the first group of Jews had returned to Jerusalem from their exile. By now the rebuilding of the city is complete. In fact we are told in Nehemiah 8 – 10 (which is useful background material to Malachi) that when the reconstruction of the walls, the temple and everything was complete, Ezra the scribe read the law of God (probably to these very Jews, or at least to their parents). And they were brought to tears by the reading of God's word. They collectively confessed their earlier sins and made a solemn promise in writing, signed by all their leaders, that in future they would be true to the covenant which God had made with Israel. There would be no more compromise with paganism; no more disobeying the Ten Commandments; no more neglect of God's temple. From now on they were going to do right what their forefathers had so conspicuously failed to do right.

Their promise had not been without effect; there were indeed no more altars to Baal among them, no more cult prostitutes to Ashtaroth, no more child sacrifices to Moloch. All those abominations were past. The temple of Jehovah was once again the religious centre of the Jewish community. No-one would have dreamed of abandoning that temple now. They had built it with their own bare hands.

And yet, in spite of all their piety, Malachi is not satisfied. With the insight of a prophet, he can detect a new form of spiritual failure in the people. Not the gross and obvious sort of apostasy that characterized the pre-exilic period, but a subtle invasive weed growing up in the midst of God's vineyard nevertheless; a weed that could grow and blossom, even in the midst of their apparent orthodoxy.

In these four morning studies we are going to identify some of the symptoms of that malaise. Tomorrow in 1:6 – 2:9 we shall hear Malachi bemoaning the *apathy* the people displayed in regard to public worship: they attended the temple, but they made sure their religion did not cost them too much. One gets the distinct impression that for many of them, public worship had become a tedious and mechanical routine. And to make matters worse, the clergy were encouraging them in this lukewarm, lackadaisical attitude.

Next, in 2:10–16, we shall find Malachi addressing the *infidelity* of the people in their domestic lives. Not necessarily the sort of infidelity that issues in adulterous relationships, though there may have been some instances of that. No, these Jews simply did not demonstrate any spiritual commitment to God in their family life. They went to the temple, but that was where it ended. So, for example, they were not bothered about the religious affiliation of their marital partners. 'My wife is a pagan – so what? Everyone will get to heaven in the end. You've got to live and let live. It doesn't matter what you believe so long as you are sincere.'

Doubly disturbing for Malachi was the fact that the divorce rate was also escalating. People were dumping their marital partners in the way you might dump an old car to make way for a newer, more attractive model. In neither of these areas – choosing a pagan partner or abandoning an existing partner – were the people of God showing the least sensitivity to what God thought about their behaviour.

Then finally in 2:17 – 4:6 we shall see Malachi putting his finger on the prevailing *cynicism* of their general moral behaviour. They were becoming sceptical about the whole business of right and wrong.

'Look,' they were saying, 'people get away with murder in this world. It's all very well for old-fashioned preachers like Malachi to waffle all that theology about God's justice – but let's face it, God has created a thoroughly unjust world. There's no profit-margin in goodness. Look at us: we have left our homes in Babylon, cashed in our life savings, come back here to Jerusalem to work on a building site, and why?

Because prophets like Malachi told us God was going to renew the old kingdom of David in all its glory, that's why.

'And what have we got for all our pain? We've got a third-rate temple that would make us a laughing stock if we'd built it in Babylon; we've got a jerry-built city wall that would have a hard job keeping out a troop of Boy Scouts, and we've got empty stomachs half the time. The economy is not picking up. The dream just hasn't materialized. The kingdom of David hasn't arrived. We are still political pawns of the Persian Empire. We have no real freedom; the wealth and the power lie in the hands of our enemies – pagan enemies, who couldn't care less about Jehovah, the God of Israel. Yet they're the ones with money in their pockets! A God of justice? Don't make me laugh! "Do others before they do you," that's the moral philosophy that works.'

Let me repeat: these are not blatant unbelievers with whom Malachi is dealing. They are church-goers, people who pride themselves on their religion. This is the seed-bed from which the Judaism we meet 400 years later in the time of Jesus was to sprout. These are not idolaters. If anything, they are incipient scribes and Pharisees. Yet there is apathy in their public worship, infidelity in their domestic relationships, and cynicism in their moral attitudes.

Such attitudes, I suggest, are far from uncommon among the people of God. In fact they are typical second-generation temptations. In the early days of any movement of spiritual renewal among God's people the danger is always fanaticism: zeal can all too easily be perverted into error as people go over the top in their new-found spiritual enthusiasm; and heresies, cults and sectarian divisions are often the result. But once the first flush of that early excitement dies away and the battle for theological orthodoxy has been won, then a new danger starts to emerge: the 'second-generation' temptation to complacency, to compromise, to worldliness, to indifference.

You can see that story repeated over and over again. Every new denomination that has ever emerged in church history was, in its infancy, an attempt – often a laudable and necessary one – to rediscover the enthusiasm, purity and commitment of the apostolic age. They read the book of Acts, they looked at the church around, and said, 'It is not like that any longer: we must make it like that.' And every denomination, in the wake of that early pristine devotion, has discovered the perils of second-generation half-heartedness. Disillusionment sets in, our fond dreams do not materialize, our triumphalism is drowned by the icy water of realism. And, just like Malachi's audience, we start to doubt as a result.

That was the root of their spiritual malaise: doubt. Not the sort of doubt that questions the existence of God, but the sort of doubt that questions whether it is really worth the effort to worship him; that questions what profit there is in being a Christian, with all the effort it involves; that questions whether the Bible really does bring blessing to those who obey it; that questions whether God cares in the least for those whom he calls his people. And there are many among evangelical Christians today who walk the same dangerous path.

In the earlier part of this century it was the battle for truth that was critical. The inspiration of Scripture, the atoning significance of the cross, the deity of Jesus – those were the cardinal issues. But for most evangelicals those battles are now fought and won. We are committed to an orthodox confession of faith. Most of us are embedded in a theological tradition that in its biblicism cannot be faulted. And yet, just like these post-exilic Jews, we can still make the cardinal mistake of resting on our laurels.

For some of us, I suspect, the passion of our spiritual youth has decayed into mid-life spiritual inertia. It shows perhaps in our attitude to worship, as it did among these Israelites. We go to church, but once a week on a Sunday morning is quite enough with a schedule like ours. We sometimes take a look at our Bibles, but habits of personal prayer and Bible study have become undisciplined – when was the last time we spent much time with God on our own? And though we still manage to show a certain amount of emotional engagement in our choruses and our songs while we are worshipping together in public, maybe the words 'What a burden it all is!' sometimes hover, if not on our lips, then at the back of our minds.

It shows too in our attitude to family life. 'What does it matter if I go out with a non-Christian?' says the Christian Union member. 'So my wife and I are getting divorced – what does it matter? It's not the unforgivable sin, is it?' says the church member.

It shows, perhaps most of all, in our attitude to moral action generally. Evangelical preachers of an earlier generation used to talk a great deal about 'holiness', about the need for a thorough moral repentance in our lives. They preached the law as well as the gospel. They preached the need for church discipline as well as church growth. They wanted to see people sanctified as well as justified, discipled as well as converted.

But today I detect a cosier and less disturbing spirit abroad in our evangelical churches, one more at ease with the values of the secular world. It is a spirit that wants to identify with evangelical Christianity, but lacks the whole-hearted commitment that authentic biblical faith demands of those who would profess it. In short, I detect doubt.

It's not the kind of doubt that denies the creed – we can be vitriolic about the Bishop of Durham when we want to be – but the sort of doubt that is unwilling to give one hundred per cent. It is not the doubt of the atheist, but that of the nominal Christian; that questions not whether it is true, but whether it is important; not whether God exists, but whether he is really worth the effort – whether, at the end of the day, faith makes a difference.

What then is the answer to this insidious, second-generation half-heartedness? How do you restore enthusiasm and motivation in spiritual things to people who have grown weary and disillusioned in their profession of faith?

The temptation, I suppose, is to address the symptoms. You can counter the apathy by whipping up more emotion in public worship, by putting a stronger beat in the choruses perhaps. You can counter the infidelity in domestic life by getting IVP to publish a good book on sex and marriage.

You can counter the rise in divorce rates by getting some Christian pressure group organized to campaign for stricter divorce laws and so forth. You can counter the moral cynicism of the church by carting everybody off to Keswick, or to Spring Harvest, for some good holiness teaching. Best of all, of course, organize a mission! If you cannot have true piety, you can at least have plenty of evangelistic activity in the church.

Malachi certainly does deal with a number of specific symptoms, as we shall be seeing in subsequent studies. But what I want you to notice very carefully is this: *that is not where he begins*. His response to the compromise and the complacency of God's people is far more radical than merely to address the outward symptoms of failure. In these opening verses he goes to the root of the problem, the root of the doubt that was feeding their lack of commitment.

God's special love

'"I have loved you," says the LORD.'

I want you to notice that Malachi is not talking here about God's general love for all people. He is speaking about God's special love for his own people: 'I have loved *you*, my chosen people.' For the root of their complacency, their indifference, infidelity, cynicism and apathy, lay in the fact that they did not really believe that God did love them or even care about them. Their adversities had destroyed their assurance of God's personal commitment to them. So Malachi sees his first task as a prophet to be that of reassuring them of the indestructible covenant love of God.

'"I have loved you," says the LORD. "But you ask, 'How have you loved us?'"'

'"Was not Esau Jacob's brother?" the LORD says. "Yet I have loved Jacob, but Esau I have hated, and I have turned his mountains into a wasteland and left his inheritance to the desert jackals"'(1:2–3).

We have already observed that the recent history of the Jews had been traumatic. Their homeland had been devastated by the Babylonian invasion. The temple had been destroyed. Most of the population had been exiled. It had been a crippling blow to their national pride.

Their sense of humiliation had not been eased by the fact that their neighbour Edom had not suffered the same fate. In fact, as the little book of Obadiah tells us, the Edomites had derived great personal satisfaction from Israel's catastrophe, and had exploited her military weakness to settle some old scores. The Edomites were the descendants of Esau, Jacob's brother, and there had been bad blood between these two tribes ever since the very early days when Jacob had cheated his older brother out of their father Isaac's blessing. So as far as the Edomites were concerned, when the Babylonian army stormed Jerusalem the Israelites were finally getting what they deserved. They were elated at the prospect of the Israelites' economic and political misery and they did everything they could to rub salt into the wound.

For the Jews, of course, that simply added insult to injury. How could God – their God, the God of Jacob – stand idly by and let the sons of Esau gloat over the misfortunes of Jacob's sons? It was a cruel and treacherous stab in the back! How could they go on believing that the covenant God was faithful to them?

And yet Malachi insists that God *is* faithful, and that they can and they must believe in his faithfulness. If only they would open their eyes to the working of his providence, they would realize how much he loved them. After all, just look at what has happened to Edom now!

'Esau I have hated. I have turned his mountains into a wasteland and left his inheritance to the desert jackals,' God said.

This is a reference to what happened in the century following the Babylonian conquest. Though Edom escaped the punitive treatment by the Babylonians, another very aggressive people had in due course overrun Edomite territory; and now Edom was in a far worse condition than Israel. The Israelites had been invited by the Persian emperor to return to their homeland and reoccupy it; but no such decree had been made for the Edomites. On the contrary, their land was a ruin. No national resurrection was scheduled for them, said the Lord.

> Edom may say, 'Though we have been crushed, we
> will rebuild the ruins.'
>
> But this is what the LORD Almighty says, 'They
> may build, but I will demolish. They will be called
> the Wicked Land, a people always under the wrath
> of the LORD. You will see it with your own eyes and
> say, "Great is the LORD – even beyond the borders
> of Israel!"' (1:4–5)

Malachi, then, insists that the Jews were doubting God's
special love for them only because they were looking at
events in the short term. If they wanted to understand what
was happening to them they must remove the myopic dis-
torting lenses from their eyes and see God's purpose
through long-distance glasses. They must cultivate a
broader perspective on events. Yes, God had punished
Israel for her sins: but he had not consigned Israel to permanent destruction. Yes, he had disciplined them, but he
had not abandoned them. As Malachi will record later on in
his prophecy, 'I the Lord do not change. So you, O descendants of Jacob, are not destroyed' (3:6).

This then is the central thrust of Malachi's prophecy, the
context for everything else he is going to teach us over these
four days. '"I have loved you," says the LORD.' Do not
doubt it. Certainly you can point to plenty of unbelievers
who seem to be having a much easier time than you are
having right now. 'So what?' asks Malachi. 'It's all purely
temporary.' For to be outside the covenant people of God is
to be under God's judgment. It is to stand in danger, not
only of his chastening hand, but of his everlasting judicial
anger. What could be worse than that? Any blessing the
world may think it now enjoys, Malachi tells us, is going to
be proved in the final analysis to be very ephemeral and
shallow. This universe will witness the vindication of God's
people. Believe in it! How can you doubt it, when God has
said, 'I have loved you'?

If you are a Christian, God says the same to you. No
matter how much pain you may have had to endure, no
matter how much humiliation you may feel you have

suffered, God says to you and to me just as he said to his prophet Malachi and the Israelites, 'I have loved you.'

What does Paul say in his letter to the Ephesians? 'He chose us in [Christ] before the creation of the world . . . In love he predestined us to be adopted as his sons . . . in accordance with his pleasure and will' (Eph. 1:4–5).

Make no mistake about it, our conscious awareness of that special, electing, eternal love is the root of all true Christian commitment. It is the fuel that stokes all true Christian enthusiasm. Christianity is not a legalistic duty, a tedious routine in which we are driven by guilt or habit or mere tradition. Christianity is a joyous celebration of an unshakeable divine affection for us. '"I have loved you," says the LORD.' Do you believe that?

A young couple were to be married. A few days before the wedding the young man was becoming a little nervous about the huge promises he was expected to make. So he went for some fatherly advice to one of the older church members who had been married for many years. 'Tell me,' he asked, 'in all those years you have been married, have you never contemplated divorce?'

The old man thought for a few moments, then replied, 'Divorce, never. Murder – often!'

Perhaps that comes close to what God feels about us. Yes, he is rough with us sometimes; but that is precisely because he loves us. Whatever happens, he will not be separated from us; he is determined to take us to glory.

The implications of love

Consider with me then a few implications of this remarkable opening statement. 'I have loved you.' What does it mean?

First let me say what it does *not* mean.

No elitism

It does not mean that there is any excuse for elitism among the people of God.

That danger has always existed, of course. The Jews have fallen into it at times. The Christian church in South Africa has done so too in certain respects. All Christians are vulnerable to the danger of treating God's covenant as the ground for some kind of racist arrogance. Put that idea out of your head; it is quite illegitimate. For the fact is, as Paul affirms on this very issue in Romans 2, God does not show favouritism.

In that connection it is important not to misunderstand the phrase, 'Esau I have hated.' The Hebrew language often exaggerates to make a point. Technically it is called 'hyperbole'. Jesus used it once in Luke 14:26, when he said that anyone who comes to him must 'hate' his father and his mother. Can you imagine Jesus encouraging hate? But he was a Hebrew and he was used to using Hebrew hyperbole. He did not mean, of course, that Christians should literally detest their parents, as his own attitude to Mary so conspicuously proves. But it was a vivid, idiomatic way of saying, 'There must be absolutely no condition or hesitation about your devotion to me. You must love me above everything else.'

A boy might very easily say something similar to his girlfriend.

'You have been making eyes at that Julia Jones,' she might say to him accusingly.

'Rubbish,' he replies. 'I can't stand the sight of Julia Jones.'

The truth is that Julia Jones might be a very attractive young lady, but he says, 'I cannot stand the sight of her', because he wants to reinforce his affirmation of devotion to his own true love.

In the same way, the Bible insists God loves the world. The psalmist says God is good to all, loving to all he has made. But he has a special love, a unique covenant love for his own people; a love which he does not share with the world at large.

A special responsibility

With the privilege of that special love comes also a special responsibility; a responsibility to be holy in the world, and to be a witness to the world. Israel had that privilege and that responsibility. When she failed in it God judged her harshly. As the prophet Amos records, 'You only have I chosen out of all the families of the earth, and that is why I am going to punish you for all your sins' (*cf.* Am. 3:2). In other words, precisely because you are special to me, I am going to be specially careful to punish you when you go wrong.'

Anyone who thinks that God showed partiality to the Jews should re-read those tortured passages from the book of Lamentations describing the Babylonian siege of Jerusalem. Indeed, anyone who thinks that God shows partiality toward the Jews ought to look again at the photos of Belsen and Auschwitz. Israel was never God's pampered pet. If she interpreted the covenant that way, history has disillusioned her and rightly so. Israel was not God's favourite, and neither, in that sense, is the church. In every age, the people of God are his chosen vehicle to carry forward his purpose to the world at large. Yes, they have his word, but their responsibility is to obey it. Yes, they have a special covenant relationship with him, but their responsibility is to welcome others into that relationship.

As someone has put it, the church is the only organization that exists for the sake of its non-members. The people of God exist for the sake of the world. The promise to Abraham was that through his seed all nations would be blessed. And Peter in the New Testament confers that role upon Christians: 'You are a chosen people, you are a holy nation, you are a people belonging to God' – why? 'that you may declare the praises of him who called you out of darkness into his wonderful light' (*cf.* 1 Pet. 2:9).

When God says, 'I love you', then, it is not to feed any elitist arrogance in us but to feed our missionary calling. Esau was outside the covenant, but there would be sons of Esau gathered around the throne on that last day, just as there will be people drawn out of every other tribe and nation and kindred. And how will they be there? Because the people of God have shown them the holiness of God and preached to them the love of God.

No spiritual pride

Again, it is all too easy to interpret the special love of God as grounds for spiritual pride. Perhaps your reaction when you hear God saying, 'I love you, but Esau I have hated' is to think how arbitrary it seems. There are the sons of Esau being allowed to plunge on their reckless route to hell, but God has arrested me. He has allowed me to discover spiritual life, he has opened my eyes, by some miracle he has awakened faith in my heart. Why me?

Every child of God asks that question. It is inevitable that they should; every child of God is *meant* to ask it. But the vital thing we have to realize is that there is no answer to it. God told Israel what his reasons for choosing them were *not*. 'I did not choose you because you were a bigger nation than any other, in fact you are one of the littlest. And I did not choose you because you were a better nation than any other, because you are one of the worst' (*cf.* Dt. 7:7). But never, never did he tell them why he had chosen them.

In fact immediately we start to speculate about the answer to the question 'Why me?' we create a heresy. To answer it is invariably to generate a false anti-Christian religion of good works and spiritual pride. To answer it is to destroy grace. Why did he love me? 'Well, he loved me because I am a good person . . . because I go to church . . . because I have been baptized.' Or, of course for the evangelical, 'He loved me because I put my hand up at an evangelistic meeting. I went forward and made my decision. I signed my name on a little card. I prayed the prayer with the counsellor.'

No, no, *no!* God's love is not a response to any merit found or foreseen in us. It is a unilateral act of his own grace. It is unconditional, free and generous. The correct answer to the question 'Why me?' is not any sentence that begins 'Because, I . . . .' There is only one correct response, and it is, 'Thank you. I did not deserve your love, I had no claim upon it, I could not earn it, I cannot repay it. But you, Lord, out of your sovereign choice, have bestowed it upon me; and I am moved to the depths of humble gratitude by your generosity in doing so.' Do any of us understand why someone should love us? Do we understand why our husband or wife loves us? The whole point about love is that we do not know why.

Beware of spiritual pride, then. A halo only has to slip a few inches to become a noose. What does the apostle Paul say? 'God chose the foolish things of the world to shame the wise' (1 Cor. 1:27). Lowly and despised things, mere nothings, to bring to nothing those who think they are something. Why? So that there may be no boasting in his presence. That is the key. There will be no boasting in glory, nobody sticking their thumbs in their golden waistcoats saying, 'Didn't I do well?'

No. We will be there because he loved us, and God knows why. We are not required to understand this love, to rationalize or justify it; but to accept it, believe it, trust it.

The difference love makes

What difference should it make to the Jews to whom Malachi speaks, what difference to us, that we trust God's word when he says, 'I have loved you'? I am almost embarrassed by the number of avenues of application that suggest themselves. Let me give you just a couple.

Self-esteem

If we really believe that we have been loved by God in this way, it will mean we can have great dignity even in the midst of trouble and adversity. These Jews were cringing, complaining, and whining, because they thought Edom had had a better deal than themselves. But in fact, says Malachi, it is Edom who deserves their pity.

The same is true of us. There are an awful lot of people in the church who suffer from what psychologists call 'low self-esteem'. They wallow in self-pity, just as these Jews were doing. They tell you they are worth nothing. You can never pay them a compliment, because they invariably assume you do not really mean it. On the other hand, they leap at any opportunity to construe any comment as a possible criticism. Haven't you met people like that? The church is full of them. Perhaps, if you are honest, you recognize yourself as one. There is at least a strand of vulnerability to low self-esteem in most of us. But it is unnecessary.

For if you are a Christian, God loves you. That is no trite platitude to be stuck in a car windscreen. It is the truth of our existence. God loves us. The trouble with our world is that we have trivialized the words, 'I love you.' Love has become a romantic vapour of the emotions, a sentimental measles which people catch and then recover from. We fall in and out of love. And that is sad, for it means love is not something people can rely on any more. 'Till death us do part' – more likely, 'Till the judge us do part.' Love in the twentieth century has become a fair-weather friend: love for better, but not for worse. Consequently our world is full of people disillusioned about love.

But that is not how God uses the vocabulary of love. For him, love is no casual affair, no wild adventure. For him, love is promise and covenant. For him, love is a moral commitment to a quality of relationship which he is determined will last for ever. That is what he means by love: 'I have loved you with an everlasting love,' he says.

Now, how can you know that you are loved like that, and then run yourself down in a self-pitying inferiority complex?

I read once of a college student in the days of the Black Power movement in the United States. This young negro had found his own way of handling the problem of racial discrimination. He had a banner on his wall that said: 'I'm black, and I'm OK, 'cause God don't make junk.'

God does not love junk, either. Is that not a reason then for every believer to hold his or her head up high?

I am reminded of the story of the little boy who was being jeered at in the playground by his peers, because they had discovered he was adopted. Eventually he rounded on them. 'All right,' he said, 'so I am adopted. All I know is, my parents chose me, but yours couldn't help having you.'

Every Christian can say the same: 'God chose me.' In the mists of eternity past he saw me, loved me and determined to save me. Of course, he may sometimes discipline me. What good parent does not? But he will never abandon me.

Perhaps, as for the heartbroken parents in the illustration with which we began, there is something in your life which is a root of bitterness between you and God. You have suffered a grievous disappointment, a broken engagement, a failed marriage, a bereavement. Maybe you have been made redundant, maybe you have failed a vital exam. Well, it is not for the Christian to wallow in demoralized self-pity. You are loved by God. You have dignity, you had better believe it. And if you do not feel that dignity, it is no wonder that your enthusiasm for spiritual things is on the wane.

Holiness

If we know we are loved by God in this special way, we will also have a hunger for holiness. 'I have loved you, you are special to me' – and therefore, you must be different.

That is the repeated logic of the Bible. There is an invisible line separating God's people from the world. It is the line defined by his love, his special relationship with his people. Anything that blurs that line will bring the world into the church and the church into the world. If the people of God are compromising with the world it is ultimately because they have forgotten who they are; they have lost the consciousness of their distinctive call. They have forgotten that the king of the universe has loved them with a special love. If the world is in your heart, it is because you need to hear again that God has loved you. You – in particular! How can we treat his worship half-heartedly, if we know he has loved us? How can we treat his covenant law so loosely when it matters so much to him? How can we speak such blasphemy as to suggest that he will let the wicked escape without punishment?

A strong sense of the special love of God for his people is the root of all gospel holiness. Walk worthy of your calling; Paul says it again and again. If we knew who we were, the world would be no threat to us. We would not be afraid to behave differently from other people. We would not fear to be called old-fashioned or narrow. We would know ourselves to be God's people, and the assurance of his love would nerve us against all those secular pressures that

27

would seek to conform us to the ways of the world. Here is the source of that hunger for holiness, which so many in this second generation of our evangelical movement seem to lack: God says, 'I have loved you.'

God has loved you; how much do you love him?

If you have done any pastoral counselling you will know all too well that marriages break down in one of two fundamentally different ways. Sometimes it is through unfaithfulness. An adulterous relationship is involved.

Often, however, marriages do not shatter under the attack of external sexual attraction in that way. They die slowly from within. Imperceptibly, by degrees, husband and wife drift apart, affection cools, communication dries up, until suddenly to their horror they discover they have become strangers living in the same house. No third party is necessarily implicated at all. The couple have been utterly faithful (in the technical sense) to each other, but sadly – in the latter years of their marriage at any rate – a chill has descended on their relationship. It was a case of faithful, yes, but frigid.

And what is true of marriages is lamentably also sometimes true of Christians. The church is not called the bride of Christ for nothing. He expects of her not simply a dutiful fidelity but a loving attachment. Sometimes with the passing of the years, the fidelity remains preserved in our doctrinal formulae and our denominational traditions. But the warmth ebbs away; and so churches lose the spark of devotion. They die slowly from within. Not for lack of doctrine, but for lack of love. That is exactly what was happening in Ephesus, of whom Christ complained at the very end of the New Testament: 'You have forsaken your first love' (Rev. 2:4). Would he say the same of us?

Christianity is not about loving the creed, it is not even about loving the Bible. Christianity is about loving Christ. We love the Bible because it tells us about him, but he is the object of our faith. We embrace the truth by embracing him, because he is the truth. Once any Christian – perhaps even out of a commendable concern to define the truth – separates love of truth from the love of Christ, then no matter how excellent their theology, no matter how explicit their creed, they have lost the truth. For the truth is in Jesus, and once that truth is detached from a committment to him personally it becomes academic and desiccated and therefore erroneous, no matter how propositionally accurate it may be.

It is so important that we understand this. Christianity is not just a matter of how we think, it is a matter of how we feel toward God and he toward us. We are precious to him, he is committed to us as a husband to a wife; and when we backslide in our enthusiasm and our devotion cools, it disappoints and hurts him. He will not put up with it. He sent Israel into exile because her love had cooled. He may do the same for us, for he wants our love and he is not satisfied with anything less. He will turn our lives upside down if he thinks it will re-awaken that love in us. He will put his finger on many issues as we study Malachi, but God's intention in this book is not to harangue us and make us feel guilty about all the things we have not done.

Fundamentally, his intention is to woo us to a new devotion to him. 'I care,' he says. 'I care about you. How could you possibly suggest I do not? I have loved you. Where is your love for me?'

2

Apathy

Malachi 1:6 – 2:9

I want to read to you from a letter written about thirty years ago, from a young Latin American student to his fiancée, to explain to her why he was breaking off their engagement.

> We have a high casualty rate. We get shot, lynched, jailed, slandered, fired from our jobs. We live in virtual poverty. We give away every penny we make above what is absolutely necessary to keep us alive. We do not have time for movies or concerts. We are described as fanatics; perhaps we are, for our lives are dominated by one great over-shadowing cause. This is the one thing about which I am in dead earnest. It is my life, my business, my hobby, my sweetheart. I work for it in the daytime and dream of it at night. I cannot carry on any friendship, or love affair, or even conversation, without relating it to this force which drives and guides my life.

That young man had been converted to Marxism.

People sometimes ask me what it is about left-wing politics that is so attractive, especially to students in the developing world; for intellectually, they point out, Marxist philosophy has more holes than a garden sieve. Its economic theories have conspicuously failed, its political predictions have invariably proved false, its violent revolutions have indisputably misfired. How can any intelligent person still believe in it?

The answer, of course, is that Marxism has never appealed primarily to the mind but to the heart. 'Nothing great in this world', wrote Emerson, 'is ever achieved without enthusiasm.' Too true; the hallmark of every great revolutionary movement in the world has been that it is able to awaken passion in people. Merely capturing academic interest is never enough, because the strongest springs of our human motivation are wound on the wheel of our emotional, rather than our intellectual, life.

You may want to argue that it ought not to be so; if so, you have a case. Emotion detached from reason is fanaticism, as that young Latin American almost recognized, perhaps, in his letter. Yet anybody who wants to change the world, especially if by harnessing the energies of the young, must reckon with this basic fact of human nature. It is the emotional dimension that drives people and gives them enthusiasm for the task. And our problem, at least in the western world, is that in large measure we have lost that passion. Back in the 1950s John Osborne, the original angry young man, wrote a play, *Look Back in Anger*. Some of the lines from it are interesting:

> 'How I long for a little ordinary human enthusiasm. Just enthusiasm – that's all. I want to hear a warm thrilling voice cry out, "Hallelujah! Hallelujah! I'm alive!"'
>
> 'Oh brother, it's such a long time since I was with anybody who got enthusiastic about anything.'

Osborne is identifying a sense of disillusionment, particularly among young people in the second half of our century. Modern men and women are in the grip of a mental inertia so severe it is in danger of anaesthetizing their drive. The prevalent attitude is 'I couldn't care less'; that is the motto of the late twentieth century, and I fear it may prove to be our epitaph. We are a tired, apathetic culture.

'Apathy' is a word originally coined by the Stoic philosophers of Greece. For them it expressed their grim determination not to allow their feelings to jeopardize their inner tranquillity. The Stoic said, 'By an effort of my will, I am determined not to be bothered.' There was something courageous, almost noble about that Stoic apathy, even if it did tend to make them rather cold people. But for us today apathy is not a virtue cultivated by such disciplined mental effort. For us, apathy is a state of lassitude born of dis-illusionment and bored indifference: not 'I won't be both-ered', but 'I can't be bothered.'

Thirty years ago, left-wing politics provided at least the illusion for some that there might be something worth bothering about. 'Maybe the enthusiasm of my youth', said that young Latin American student, 'can be channelled into something.' Marxism, for all its crazy theories, at least had the power to excite and inflame. It had a self-assurance that demanded sacrifice. It had a dream which, no matter how spurious, could give young lives purpose and hope. Little wonder that a Latin American student of the 1960s was willing to sacrifice his marriage to his Marxism. But the tragedy is that thirty years on, even Marxism has become a broken reed. Not even a fanatic can continue to believe in it.

Even as early as the end of the 1960s, graffiti were appearing in students' toilets around Europe expressing disillusionment with left-wing philosophy. One of the most famous read:

> 'To do is to be' – Sartre
> 'To be is to do' – Camus
> 'Do-be-do-be-do' – Frank Sinatra

When I was at university many of my friends were very radical left-wingers. Many of them are now bank managers and such like. One of my great heroes when I was a sixth-former was a particularly left-wing revolutionary thinker. Now (as I discovered about ten years ago to my chagrin) he runs a Paris boutique.

Apathy – a church's crisis

Yet sadly the greatest tragedy in the wake of this collapse of credibility in Marxist revolutionary politics has been that so few of these disillusioned young men and women from the sixties and early seventies have found a new focus for their enthusiasm in the church of Jesus Christ. Why is that? Because, all too often, the church of Jesus Christ has sold out to apathy too. The church of the twentieth century, at least in the West, has lost its zeal.

Some years ago, attending a conference on church growth, I was rather amused to find that one of the major questions being addressed was, 'Why are the mainstream denominations in Britain all declining numerically?' One of the preliminary pre-conference exercises had been a survey of church attendance, to determine whether statistics and graphs could shed any light on this situation. I was amused at the irony, for I suspect that the survey was symptomatic of the disease they were trying to identify.

Once any group or movement starts analysing its failures with statistics and graphs, it is a sure sign that it is on its death-bed. It has lost its vigour and confidence. It is like a hypochondriac, who pores over medical charts but never recognizes that the real cause of his malaise is in that negative and morbid attitude which moved him to look at those charts in the first place.

So the church in the late twentieth century has called in the sociologists, when the rot lies in the grassroots of the Christian movement. We have lost our passion. People used to talk about the church 'militant', but we have abdicated that word to the left-wing politicians. The average church member today is more emotionally involved in his football team than in the kingdom of God. He or she is more moved by the latest soap opera than by the gospel of Christ. Like those Laodiceans of old, we are neither hot nor cold. We are just tepid, lukewarm, half-hearted Christians. In a word – apathetic.

The apathy of God's people

In that respect we are remarkably similar to the people of God in the days of Malachi, for they had become apathetic. A 'couldn't care less' casualness infected every aspect of their spirituality, nowhere more obviously than in their attitude to public worship.

See how God speaks to them here.

'You have shown contempt for my name.' How? 'You placed defiled food on my altar.' How have we defiled it?

'By saying that the Lord's table is contemptible. When you bring blind animals for sacrifice, is that not wrong? When you sacrifice crippled or diseased animals, is that not wrong? Try offering them to your governor! Would he be pleased with you? Would he accept you?' (*cf.* 1:6–8).

The law of Moses laid down strict guidelines on the quality of animals to be used in the ritual sacrifices of the Old Testament religion. They had to be the best; you were not allowed to bring anything inferior. The animal had to be young, healthy, unblemished and perfect. But Malachi's compatriots were ignoring those rules. If they could get away with presenting a second-rate or even a third-rate animal to the priests, they did. And Malachi is outraged by it: it is the brazen impertinence of it that gets to him. Do they really think that they can deceive God with their cheap sacrifices? 'Try offering them to your governor,' he says.

Some years ago Her Majesty the Queen visited Cambridge where I live. As part of her visit, local traders clubbed together to provide a floral tribute. Can you imagine her reaction if the Guild of Commerce had presented her with a bouquet of withered dandelions? Such a gift would have been an outrageous insult to her elevated person and office. Well, says Malachi, it is the same sort of outrage you perpetrate when you come to church. How dare you present these tatty offerings to God! Do you really expect him to be impressed by such off-hand expressions of your devotion? Do you anticipate that his mercy or his blessing is going to flow into your life, when you have so little concern to win his approval? This is not worship. This is insufferable insolence!

'"Oh, that one of you would shut the temple doors, so that you would not light useless fires on my altar! I am not pleased with you," says the LORD Almighty' (1:10).

What an appalling thing for God to have to say! Yet, says Malachi, that is how God feels about it. You would be better off going down to the pub on Sunday mornings than going to church in that frame of mind. Why, if all you are going to do is to engage in such half-hearted empty rituals, you would be better off staying in bed! Do you not realize who it is you are dealing with?

'Universalism' in Malachi

> 'My name will be great among the nations, from the rising to the setting of the sun. In every place incense and pure offerings will be brought to my name, because my name will be great among nations,' says the LORD Almighty (1:11).

We need to pause here. Those of you who have read any commentaries on Malachi will probably be aware that this verse has provoked quite a considerable amount of debate among the scholars. Many liberal interpreters of the Bible have hailed it as a thrilling affirmation of universal salvation. 'Look,' they say, 'Malachi here sees pagan worship as worship of the true God.'

Such a multi-faith pluralism, of course, is very congenial to our modern mood. The Roman Catholic theologian Karl Rahner has often insisted that other faiths are really already worshipping Christ, unwittingly, under different names. We should no longer talk about 'non-Christians', he suggests, but 'anonymous Christians', for everyone is a Christian really. John Hick, a Protestant theologian, has gone so far as to recommend that competitive proselytizing – the different world religions seeking to win converts – should be abandoned. He urges instead a combined mission on the part of all the great world religions together, in the name of some kind of common amorphous spiritual consciousness.

It comes as no surprise, when that ethos prevails in the theological establishments, that multi-faith services in our cathedrals are becoming so fashionable. Indeed, one has to wonder: if and when Prince Charles is crowned, who will be standing alongside the Archbishop of Canterbury in Westminster Abbey? – always assuming that the ceremony is held in Westminster Abbey, and not in some temple dedicated to New Age mysticism.

I shall have more to say about this subject tomorrow, because it is an issue that was of great significance to Malachi in his day as well. Suffice it to say here that verse 11 provides absolutely no grounds for that kind of universalism, though it has often been cited in support of it. It is quite unthinkable that Malachi is endorsing pagan idolatry, as if it were an acceptable expression of human spiritual awareness of the true God.

Three things at least count against such an interpretation. First of all, if you read his words carefully in verse 11, you will see that *the worship he is talking about is quite explicitly directed to the unique God of the Bible*. 'My name will be great among the nations . . . Pure offerings will be brought to my name, because my name will be great.' What name is that? Certainly not Baal, or Zeus, or Allah, or Krishna. The name Malachi is speaking of is Jehovah, the LORD. He is speaking here of worship offered to the true God.

Secondly, if Malachi were endorsing a universalist theology as these modern theologians suggest, *it would fly straight in the face of the very tough line he takes later, on mixed marriages between Jews and pagans (cf. 2:11)*. As we shall see tomorrow, he is definitely not in favour of such things. But he could hardly object to them, if he were the universalist some paint him.

But the third reason such an interpretation fails is because *it does not recognize the ambiguity of the tenses used in this verse*. The time reference of a Hebrew verse is often much more flexible than in English. The tense used in verse 11 can have a future rather than a present sense. Thus the NIV translates it, 'My name *will be* great among the nations . . . In every place offerings *will be* brought.' I am quite certain the NIV is right to do so. Malachi is not saying that worshippers of Baal and Zeus are unwittingly worshipping Jehovah under another name. He is saying that one day soon, worshippers of Baal and Zeus – indeed worshippers of every false deity this fallen world has ever invented for itself – will acknowledge the true God.

This is in fact the first hint of a very strong emphasis in Malachi on the prophetic future, the last days. Malachi *is* anticipating a universalism, but it is not the universalism of multi-faith services in Westminster Abbey, where Hindus and Muslims address Brahma and Allah in spiritual fellowship with bishops of the Christian church. No: Malachi is anticipating here the universalism of heaven, a time when the whole human race will bow the knee to one name. 'The LORD, he is God,' they will say.

Already, in exile, Malachi and other faithful Jews (such as Daniel) had proved that the God of the Bible could be acknowledged, even by pagan emperors like Nebuchadnezzar. There was even increasing evidence of proselytes coming to the Jewish faith from a Gentile background. Already books such as Ruth and Jonah warned them of the dangers of xenophobic prejudice. Their traditional enemies, the Moabites, the Assyrians and the Philistines, would one day respond to God's word. They *could* respond to God's word even now. God's purpose was wide enough to embrace them; it was not just for the Jews. And in the oracles of many of the prophets, a day when there would be a huge harvest from the Gentile nations was regularly anticipated. (If you want an extraordinary example of that, look at Isaiah 19:19-25.)

This then is Malachi's universalism. It is not the universalism of liberal theologians. It is the universalism of the Gospel of John, where we find the Master saying, 'A time is coming when you will worship the Father neither on this mountain nor in Jerusalem . . . a time is coming and has now come when the true worshippers will worship the Father in spirit and truth' (Jn. 4:21, 23). It is the universalism of the book of Acts: 'So then, God has granted even the Gentiles repentance unto life' (Acts 11:18). It is the universalism of the book of Revelation. There are no dissidents among that crowd gathered around the throne; no-one shouting, 'Let's hear it for Muhammad!', 'Three cheers for Buddha!' The whole of heaven is united around the praise of a single name: 'Jesus is Lord.'

'"My name will be great among the nations, from the rising to the setting of the sun. In every place incense and pure offerings will be brought to my name, because my name will be great among the nations," says the LORD Almighty.' It will happen, says Malachi: and yet you Jews, who of all people should be giving God the glory for his unique, incomparable, sovereign lordship over the entire world – you dare to treat his public worship with indifference, with apathy! You are not doing God any favours by worshipping him, you know. He does not need your pathetic gifts. He is the Lord of the cosmos, the great king who one day will be revered by everyone.

'But you profane [his name] by saying of the Lord's table, "It is defiled", and of its food, "It is contemptible." And you say, "What a burden!" and you sniff at it contemptuously,' says the LORD Almighty' (1:12–13).

Many commentators suggest that the picture Malachi is portraying for us in the phrase 'sniff at it' is of these Jews turning up their noses disdainfully at the sacrificial offerings they were having to bring. But the Hebrew verb actually means to exhale rather than to inhale. So I wonder if the picture is not rather that of a heavy, weary sigh rather than a sniff: a weary 'Ugh, what a fag! What a burden!'

You can just see them, can't you, looking at their watches to see how long it is all going on; fidgeting with their chorus books, counting the tassels on the high priest's robe to pass the time, wishing this tedious, boring business would all be over so that they could get their Sunday lunch. Apathy is almost too weak a word to describe the appalling lack of emotional engagement with the public worship they were performing.

The reasons for apathy

Now, what were the reasons for it? If we can identify them, maybe we will identify some of the reasons for apathy in the Christian church of the twentieth century too.

A lack of reverence for God's person

'A son honours his father, and a servant his master. If I am a father, where is the honour due to me? If I am a master, where is the respect due to me?' (1:6).

Yesterday we saw that one of the primary reasons for this half-heartedness and apathetic spirit in the people of God was that they had lost their assurance of God's love. They did not really believe in that love any longer. And that, as we saw, contributed in a major way to their spiritual half-heartedness.

But here in verse 6 Malachi sets against that their fear of God. He wants to guard against any sentimentalizing of the divine love, which might lead to a diminished respect for God's authority. 'He may love Israel, indeed he does; but you must not forget he is your sovereign master, he deserves honour' (literally, weight, gravity), 'he deserves respect' (literally, fear, or even terror or dread). So to treat God with honour and respect is the very opposite of treating him as somebody insignificant or not intimidating.

We must never let our view of the love of God distort our thinking so that we can treat him like some kind of heavenly buddy. He is a great king, to be feared among the nations; but they did not fear him. They did not treat coming into his presence with the seriousness it deserved. Instead they seem to have breezed into the temple, offering their sacrifices as if they were tipping some waiter in a cheap restaurant.

Am I not speaking the truth when I say that we too need to heed this word about the fear of God? There is a great deal said about the love of God today. It is rightly and necessarily said, but it can lead us into a sentimental view of God and we can lose our reverence. In trying to make our public services of worship user-friendly, welcoming, suitable for all the family and informal, there is the danger too that we no longer communicate to one another and to ourselves the awsomeness of God. Partly, I suppose, it is cultural. We are not used to showing ordinary human beings honour and respect any longer, are we?

A group of American tourists were being shown round the Houses of Parliament. As they were being taken along one of the corridors, Lord Hailsham, who was then Lord Chancellor, appeared on his way to some civic occasion; he was dressed in his Chancellor's robes and regalia, with heavy gold chains and all the rest, and made a very impressive figure. As he approached he saw, beyond the party of tourists, the Leader of the Opposition, Mr Kinnock. Wanting to speak to him, he raised his hand and called out, 'Neil!' Whereupon all the tourists dropped to one knee.

We smile at the story because it is somehow incongruous in our modern democratic western world, to imagine people spontaneously kneeling like that to someone of higher rank. Even bowing to our sovereign the Queen has become a perfunctory nod of the head, these days, has it not? If we do not kneel to our earthly masters, it's no wonder that we do not kneel any longer to pray. I wonder if I am alone in thinking that something has been lost in the abandonment of that traditional body-language of prayer – something that would have gone some way, perhaps, to protect us from apathy. ' "If I am a father, where is the honour due to me? If I am a master, where is the respect due to me? . . . I am a great king," says the Lord Almighty, "and my name is to be feared among the nations" ' (1:6, 14).

A hypocritical spirit among the people

'Cursed is the cheat who has an acceptable male in his flock and vows to give it, but then sacrifices a blemished animal to the Lord' (verse 14). That is revealing; it shows that there is an element of pretence in what these people were doing. Like Ananias and Sapphira in the book of Acts, these Jews wanted the kudos of being known as pious people but were not prepared to pay the price such a reputation required. So they cheated and lied; they substituted knackered mutton for the prime lamb they had promised to bring to the temple.

Hypocrisy is often the partner of apathy, implying as it does a lack of genuine feeling. Do you remember those famous lines from Shakespeare's *Hamlet*?

> This above all: to thine own self be true,
> And it must follow, as the night the day,
> Thou canst not then be false to any man. (I.iii)

As a playwright, Shakespeare was more familiar than most with the business of acting a part. And as he studied human behaviour, he clearly observed that such theatricals were not confined to the stage; all too often the image we try to project of ourselves is an artificial one, one we play for the benefit of others.

Some years ago a young undergraduate in Cambridge confessed this to me very candidly. She said, 'I come from a Christian home. When I go home in the vacation I am the decent, respectable, virgin Christian daughter my parents want me to be. But when I come up to college, I become a wild, dissipated, sexually permissive junkie.' She told me, 'My real problem is I do not know which is the real me.' In fact she admitted that even in coming to see me she wondered if she wasn't just adding another role to her repertoire, that of a guilt-stricken penitent, longing for priestly absolution perhaps.

I had a lot of sympathy for that young student. For in one way or another many of us fall into the same trap of inconsistency and unreality in our lives. I explained to her that at least she had one thing on her side. In this pattern of pretence she had woven about herself, at least she was aware of what she was doing; she was suspicious of her motives, she was critical of her insincerity. At least she knew she was play-acting. At least she was still searching for some nobler stance of inward honesty. At least she still wanted above all to her own self to be true, even if she was finding it difficult.

It is a tragedy that it is not always so. There are some who fix the actor's mask so securely to their faces they forget what they really look like. Pretence becomes so habitual they are no longer conscious that it *is* pretence. They practise double standards, they live a double life, they use double talk, and by some extraordinary feat of moral blindness, they feel no pang of guilt about all this duplicity. On the contrary, they frequently contrive to be sanctimonious and self-righteous. They parade themselves as pillars of the church, even as ministers. 'The church is full of hypocrites,' jibes the man in the street. And the tragedy is that so often the reproach is true.

Beware of unreality. There is one person who, while he

watches our performance on the stage of life, is never fooled by the false images we present upon it. He sees through the façade of affectation we erect, he observes the hidden inconsistencies, he perceives the false motives, he discerns the secret fraud. He is never deceived, he knows who we really are. He knows what we are really offering, no matter what we pretend to be offering for the eyes of others. So beware of hypocrisy. There is too much of it among us, and it always conceals a secret apathy, a secret contempt for God, a secret lack of real interest in spiritual things.

A lack of responsibility on the part of the professional clergy

'It is you, O priests, who show contempt for my name' (1:6).

'This admonition is for you, O priests' (2:1).

What was wrong with the priesthood?

It might be easier to ask, what was *right* with the priesthood? For a start, the priests were colluding with the people in *the presentation of dubious and polluted offerings*. They accepted the inferior animals without question, placing them on the altar. In so doing of course they were clearly indicating to everybody that they had as little regard for God's name as anybody else.

More than that, there was *their general, shabby personal example*. A priest, according to Malachi, ought to demonstrate what real reverence for God was all about. God's special relationship with the tribe of Levi was conditional upon that. His covenant with Levi meant that life, health and peace would be mediated to the people through their priestly ministries, provided the tribe of Levi showed awe for God's name, and true instruction was found on their lips.

But these priests had violated that covenant. It was transparently obvious to everybody, from the stupefied yawns on their faces and the casual manner with which they did their business, that they were as bored with all this temple ritual as anybody else.

But most important of all, this priesthood had neglected what clearly Malachi regarded as *their chief and most important ministry* – which (perhaps contrary to our preconceived ideas about Old Testament religion) was not offering sacrifices on the altar. The primary role of the priest, says Malachi, is the teaching of God's word.

'The lips of a priest ought to preserve knowledge, and from his mouth men should seek instruction – because he is the messenger of the LORD Almighty' (2:7).

But these priests were not preachers. Oh, no doubt they wore the right vestments, they mouthed the right liturgical words; but their sermons, if they preached any at all, were just empty platitudes. Instead of challenging the general slide towards worldliness and spiritual indifference and apathy, they endorsed it.

'You . . . have shown partiality in matters of the law' (2:9).

Almost certainly Malachi means that there was no consistency, no integrity in what they preached to the people. They bent the truth so that this apathetic, half-hearted people felt secure in their way of life. Their polished sermonettes each sabbath offended nobody and converted nobody. Instead, by their endorsement of the general low standard of spirituality among God's people, they caused them to stumble. No wonder, then, that God says in 1:10 that he wishes someone would close their church doors. By leaving them open they were doing more harm than good. 'Make no mistake about it,' says Malachi, 'God will not overlook this appalling derogation of leadership responsibility. There will be no blessing upon the ministry of such shallow ministers.'

'I will send a curse upon you, and I will curse your blessings' (2:2).

In other words: the benedictions that you priests conventionally announce at the end of the service will have no effect; why should I pay attention to prayers from people who are so uninterested in their mediatorial task? When you pronounce a priestly benediction, it will have the force of a curse on these people, not a blessing. What is more, he says, I will destroy your prestige in the public eye.

'I will spread on your faces the offal from your festival sacrifices' (2:3).

'I have caused you to be despised and humiliated before all the people' (2:9).

It is always the way, of course. The world has ultimately nothing but contempt for clergy who do not live up to the standards of biblical faith and conduct they are meant to represent. We have bishops today who think they are doing us a favour by expressing scepticism about the resurrection of Jesus from the dead. They think they are improving the public image of the church, helping more people to come to church.

But if you ask the person in the street you will discover, quite to the contrary, that all such tactics do is confirm twentieth-century men and women in their utter contempt for the church. The same must be said for the scandals attaching to American TV evangelists that have hit the headlines in recent years. Such things undermine years of evangelistic endeavour. What was it Jesus said? 'If salt loses its saltiness . . . it is no longer good for anything' . . . except to be thrown out and trampled' (Mt. 5:13).

A special word to leaders

We must not underestimate the very special onus God places upon those who are called to be pastors and ministers of his flock. James advises, 'Not many of you should presume to be teachers . . . because you know that we who teach will be judged more strictly' (Jas. 3:1). If there is one thing in the Bible worse than being a sinner it is being a stumbling block. Better, said Jesus, to have a concrete necklace around your head and be dropped into the ocean, than for a person who has been a stumbling block to God's people to face God's judgment (*cf. e.g.* Mk. 9:42). Those are terrifying words on the lips of our Master, but they are words which, if we are Christian leaders, we had better not ignore.

Take heed to your life and your doctrine: that was Paul's advice to Timothy. A Christian leader is not an authoritarian figure who can boss people around. He has only two weapons in his armoury of leadership: personal example (life) and Bible teaching (doctrine). Make sure those two things have integrity.

I am not saying that being that sort of teacher, preacher or pastor will make you popular or successful. It is quite clear there was a lot of pressure on the priests in Malachi's day to be the kind of priests they were. An apathetic church wants apathetic preachers. If you tell people of the cost of discipleship, they will all too often accuse you of religious fanaticism. If you spell out the need for conversion, they will often call you a fundamentalist crank. If you speak of judgment to come, they will call you an intolerant bigot. On the other hand, if you tell people how easy the way is, all too often they will smother you with flattery. Legitimize their sin with your reshaped Christian ethics, and their faces will light up with admiration for your pastoral sensitivity. Abolish hell from your universalist theology, and they will give you university degrees.

Well did the poet Milton say: 'Truth never comes into the world, but like a bastard to the ignominy of him that brought her forth.'

All too often that is the case. But integrity is demanded of us in our personal lives and in our public teaching. Too many of us in the Christian ministry are simply not taking that responsibility seriously. Some of us are spending too much time in the office and far too little time studying. Some of us are offering our people five minutes when their spiritual condition is so appalling it needs at least fifty. Some of us think that by waving our hands over bread and wine once a week we are doing something. Some of us think that when we get into the pulpit we are there to be stand-up comics or chat-show hosts.

No. We are there to be the teachers and exemplars of the word. Our lips and our lives must tell the same message, and it must be the message of the Bible. That is what we owe our people: our holiness and our Bible teaching. If we do not give them that, we are giving them nothing, however well-organized the church is.

I am worried about the standard of ministry in evangelical churches, just as much as I am about that among those who are more liberal in their theological tradition. The trouble with these priests of Malachi's day is not that they were heretics; they were just comfortable preachers. They confirmed people in their preconceived ideas. They were conventional preachers; they never risked their public acceptability by saying anything unpopular. If anybody ever deserved the title 'conservative', these priests did.

That worries me. It worries me when people nod so vigorously in agreement with my sermons; I must be doing something wrong. It worries me, more generally, that so much preaching in our evangelical constituency is boringly predictable, that people come not to be challenged but to be confirmed in what they already know or think. It worries me that so much evangelical preaching is smug and self-assured, that so many evangelical churches are like mutual admiration societies. The real word of God always disturbs, always surprises, always shocks.

What should a priest be? 'The messenger of the LORD Almighty' (2:7). That is an astonishing title. For elsewhere in Malachi, that is his own name: it is the title of a prophet (cf. 3:1–5). Clearly, Malachi believes that a real priest should have a prophetic dimension to his ministry. Let those of us who are leaders heed the admonition of Malachi's words. We have a special responsibility for the apathy of the church.

3

Infidelity

Malachi 2:10–16

Wilt thou have this woman to thy wedded wife, to
live together after God's ordinance in the holy
estate of Matrimony? Wilt thou love her, comfort
her, honour, and keep her, in sickness and in
health; and, forsaking all other, keep thee only
unto her, so long as ye both shall live?

The man shall answer: I will.

('The Form of Solemnisation of Matrimony',
Book of Common Prayer)

Promises are important to relationships. They are important
because we human beings are so unpredictable. No matter
how long or well you know people, they never lose the
capacity to surprise you or indeed to let you down.

A prophet in the Old Testament once compared the
human race in this respect to a flock of sheep: 'We turn
every one to our own way' (*cf.* Is. 53:6). It's a very appropriate analogy.

A zoologist acquaintance of mine once wrote a doctoral
thesis on 'The Normal Walk of Animals'. He set up a course
in the laboratory equipped with various kinds of instru-
mentation to try to measure how the gait of animals differed
between species. He told me that he got excellent results
from all sorts of beasts except the sheep. No two sheep ever
walked the same way along that course. Indeed, no single
sheep ever walked that same course twice the same way.
Sheep behaviour simply was not reproducible. The sheep is
not only perverse, he discovered, it is individualistically
perverse.

According to the prophet, it shares that characteristic with
human beings. Human behaviour is always idiosyncratic; it
is not enough that we go the wrong way; to adapt Frank
Sinatra, 'We do it our way', a way different from everyone

else's. We are very original sinners. That, of course, makes life difficult. People whose behaviour cannot be predicted cannot be trusted. And without trust, human relationships are impossible.

Take marriage, for instance. Here is a relationship which, if it can be terminated on the whim of either partner, can surely never be a deep and satisfying union. Neither partner can really afford to take the emotional risk of total self-giving to the other if the thought is there all the time: 'He or she may desert me.' A marriage without promises must always be a marriage with mental reservations, vulnerable to destructive suspicions and doubts. For you dare not commit all your hopes to a person you cannot fully trust, and you cannot fully trust the person whose future responses cannot be reliably predicted.

That is why I say that promises are important to relationships. A promise is a voluntary decision to behave predictably, a way of making my responses dependable without destroying my human freedom of action. 'I will love you, comfort you, honour and keep you in all circumstances of life. I will be totally faithful to you for the rest of my life.' The husband vows this to the wife, the wife to the husband. So the relationship is no longer the victim of fickle passion; it depends now upon the truthfulness of the parties involved. The vital issue is no longer, 'Am I clever enough to predict her future behaviour?' Or 'Am I attractive enough to sustain his future interest?' The vital issue now is: 'Can I rely on my spouse's word?' The promise, by its pledge of constancy, makes possible a relationship of trust, where previously such a relationship would have been foolhardy and presumptuous.

The promises of God

Now one of the most remarkable and important things that the Bible has to teach us is that God makes promises. And those promises are vitally important in our relationship with him, for exactly the reason they are vitally important in a marriage. God's behaviour is not easily predictable either. Of course he is neither capricious nor irrational, still less sinful; but his personality is unfathomably mysterious and his purposes unimaginably complex. As Isaiah says, 'No human being ever guessed what God was up to' (cf. Is. 55:8–9). No, if we are going to depend upon God's future behaviour, it can only be because he has made a promise to us. And the wonderful truth the Bible has to share with us is that he has indeed made such promises.

The Bible calls them 'covenants', and the most important covenant was the one he made when he pledged to Abraham that he and his descendants would be blessed, and through them all the nations of the world would be blessed too. In the years after that promise was given, of course, the children of Abraham, the Jews, encountered all kinds of ups and downs in their historical experience. There were many occasions when God chastened them, when they experienced judgment at his hand. And yet the prophets of Israel never lost their confidence in the special relationship their nation had with God. Why? Because it was based on a promise. They could not always understand what God was doing. But they were convinced that God's relationship with Israel was permanent, because it was based on covenant love.

We have seen an example of that already at the very beginning of this book of Malachi.

'"I have loved you," says the LORD.'

He is not talking there about God's general love for everybody. He is talking about his special, covenant love for the sons of Jacob.

Two things follow from this fundamental revelation in the Bible of God as one who makes covenants. The first is that *God is faithful*. A promise is no use at all if you cannot depend upon it. But God's word can be depended upon. As Moses said in Deuteronomy 7, he is the faithful God who keeps his covenant of love.

The second consequence, which is closely related to the first, is this: that *God requires faithfulness of us*. Faithfulness, that is, in our vertical relationship to him; faithfulness also in our horizontal relationships with one another. That of course is why Jesus, when asked to summarize God's law, said there are just two things involved: love God, love your neighbour. Covenant love works both ways. According to the Bible, we human beings are intended by God to live relationally in a covenant relationship with God and with one another – to love him, to love one another; and to do so reliably. The sure route to all divine blessing and all social harmony, indeed to heaven itself, is faithfulness – behaviour that can be trusted, because it is based on a promise. On the other hand, the sure route to divine cursing, to social anar-chy, the sure route in fact to hell, is infidelity – behaviour that cannot be trusted, because it will not be bound by promise.

Sadly, we discover that it was that second route, the route of infidelity, which the Jewish people seemed determined to take in the days of Malachi.

The infidelity of the people

'Have we not all one Father? Did not one God create us? Why do we profane the covenant of our fathers by breaking faith with one another?' (2:10).

Notice that phrase: 'breaking faith'. Look down the chapter and you will find it occurs again and again: in verses 10, 11, 14, 15 and finally at the very end, in verse 16: 'Guard yourself in your spirit, and do not break faith.'

For breaking faith is exactly what Israel was doing. She was sinking in a sea of spiritual half-heartedness and moral declension, and the fundamental reason was that she was not willing to face up to the demands of covenant love. She did not believe in such covenant love towards her from God; and, because she did not believe in it, she was not practising it. Vertically she was being unfaithful to God; horizontally her people were being unfaithful to one another.

Left unremedied, such a situation spelt certain disaster. So, in our passage this morning, Malachi appeals to them to reconstruct this fundamental moral commitment to faithful-ness at the centre of their lives. 'Listen,' he says, 'Do you not realize that by very nature we are bound together in a covenant relationship? Have we not all one father?'

Is he speaking of one 'Father' (that is God), or 'father' (that is, Abraham or even Adam)? Well, the commentators differ.

Perhaps he is being deliberately ambiguous, alluding to both the vertical and the horizontal components of this covenant relationship simultaneously. Either way, he is saying this: 'We are a covenant people. We owe a debt, a duty of fidelity to God and one another. Why then are we profaning that covenant by breaking faith?'

He illustrates with two specific examples, and both centre on marriage and family life. The first, in verses 11 and 12, concerns the taking of pagan partners in marriage. The second, in verses 13–16, is about the divorcing of marital partners.

Malachi then is no longer talking about public worship. He is now turning his searchlight upon the much more private, intimate sphere of the home. He is saying, 'Listen – God is just as interested in what is happening in your domestic affairs as in what is happening up at the temple. Don't think you can compartmentalize your life, keeping your religion and your private lives in separate boxes. On the contrary! God insists upon a full integration of your spirituality into every area of your life. So it is no good going up to the temple offering sacrifices, then coming home to a pagan wife and wondering why your sacrifices bring no blessing into your life. It is no good weeping and wailing in prayer at the temple, and then coming back and divorcing your wife. God will not heed or bless those who break faith with him or with one another.'

Unfaithfulness towards God

It needs little imagination to see the immense relevance a passage like this has for us and for our society today. Let us start with Malachi's example of the taking of pagan wives.

> Judah has broken faith. A detestable thing has been committed in Israel and in Jerusalem: Judah has desecrated the sanctuary the LORD loves, by marrying the daughter of a foreign God. As for the man who does this, whoever he may be, may the LORD cut him off from the tents of Jacob – even though he brings offerings to the LORD Almighty. (2:11–12)

Let me tell you about Joe. Joe says, 'It doesn't matter what you believe, so long as you are sincere.' He is a very liberally minded, tolerant fellow. He goes to church every Sunday, but he would be the last person in the world to press his religion on anybody else, least of all his wife. 'I am sure we will all find our own way to God in the end,' he confidently affirms. 'The Hindu has his way, the Muslim has his way, I have mine and my wife has hers. But like lines of longitude on a globe, eventually we shall find that our paths converge at the same pole. How could God possibly be so intolerant as to let only Christians into heaven? What an outrageously narrow-minded idea! No: it doesn't matter what you believe, so long as you are sincere.'

And there is no denying that Joe's is an immensely attractive point of view, especially in our modern world where mosques and temples vie with churches and chapels on the High Street. But is Joe right?

Let us fantasize a little for a moment. Joe, like me, enjoys walking. One day while out for a walk he meets a hiker.

'Lovely day,' Joe says.

'Great,' replies the hiker enthusiastically. 'I am on a pilgrimage to Canterbury. They tell me there is an impressive cathedral there.'

Joe considers for a moment. He is pretty sure the road the hiker is on leads in the opposite direction. But he is not infallible, is he? And he hates to be a wet blanket on somebody else's religious enthusiasm. Surely everybody is entitled to their own opinion. If this chap really wants to get to Canterbury, that road is as good as any other, he reasons. It doesn't matter what you believe, so long as you are sincere.

Imagine another scenario. Joe works in a chemist's shop. He is not a trained pharmacist, but he packs the shelves and serves on the counter. He has picked up a little bit of knowledge about medicine. One day an elderly lady comes into the shop, clutching a box of pills.

'My friend gave me these,' she says. 'He says they will cure my arthritis. But I'm not sure how many to take. Can you help me?'

Joe looks at the unmarked box hesitantly. Privately, he is almost sure he has seen the pharmacist dispensing pills from the poisons cupboard that look remarkably similar to these. But then, what does he know about drugs? And he would hate to discourage anyone in their suffering.

'If you really think they will help you, my dear, you just take as many as you like,' he advises. After all, he reasons with himself, it doesn't matter what you believe, so long as you are sincere.

You may be saying that my imaginary encounters have caricatured Joe's position; that there is all the difference in the world between an attitude of religious tolerance and the kind of irresponsibility that knowingly recommends poisons or gives wrong directions on a journey.

But is there really any difference? At the heart of all those things, you see, there is an issue of truth at stake. To say, 'It doesn't matter what you believe, so long as you are sincere' is nonsense. You might just as well say, 'All roads lead to Canterbury,' or 'All pills treat arthritis.' Many world religions teach fundamentally disjunctive and contradictory things about God and the world. They cannot all be true, they cannot all be right. You can hold that they are all true or right only by defying all the normal rules of logic and radically redefining the very nature of truth.

The Bible will not commit such intellectual suicide. Malachi will not. And because he will not, he cannot endorse the marital choices which many of his compatriots were making.

'Judah has desecrated the sanctuary the LORD loves, by marrying the daughter of a foreign god' (2:11).

That is simply an idiomatic way of saying that it was becoming common for Jews to marry pagan women.

It is not difficult to imagine how they rationalized it. Their arguments would be very similar to Joe's. 'A person's religion is their business, that's what I say. My wife has every right to worship whatever god she pleases. It doesn't do to have a closed mind. We'll all get there in the end. I heard the Reverend Levi say so in the temple only last Sunday!' – so plausible, and yet clearly, in Malachi's eyes, so pernicious.

Do not misunderstand. There is no racist prejudice

motivating his criticisms. There is no support to be found here for apartheid race laws on marriage, or anything like that. The Old Testament is by no means as ethnocentric as some people make out. Never forget that Ruth, the girl from Moab, married a Jew and became an honoured antecedent of King David. But the point was, she embraced the God of Israel; she was a *converted* pagan. What Malachi disapproves of is the refusal of these men of Israel, who had married pagan women, to bring their homes under the authority of Jehovah.

Their marriages had lost their spiritual and religious dimension and had become mere contracts, based perhaps purely on a goal of sexual gratification. No consideration was given to the implication such an attitude would have for themselves, or for their children or for their nation. They were there in church every sabbath, but they came alone and were content to do so; it did not disturb them. They saw nothing wrong in a marriage that united two bodies without uniting two souls. For Malachi this was just one more mark of the half-heartedness which he could see spreading among the people of God in his day.

See what he calls it in verse 11: 'a detestable thing'. It is a word that is used in the book of Deuteronomy for all kinds of disgusting and disgraceful pagan practices. 'Why,' says Malachi, 'such marriages desecrate the sanctuary.' That is, they make the individual concerned unholy, so that when he comes to offer his sacrifice to God he pollutes the temple area by his presence. Such people, says Malachi, must be disciplined. They must be ostracized from the community, whatever their social standing and no matter how pious they may apparently be.

'As for the man who does this, whoever he may be, may the LORD cut him off from the tents of Jacob – even though he brings offerings to the LORD Almighty' (2:12).

This, of course, is a very tough line. And there are several things that I need to say to you by way of clarification and qualification, if we are rightly to apply these words to our situation today.

Malachi was speaking into a particular historical situation

If you read the book of Nehemiah, particularly chapter 13, you will find that in the days of Malachi (which were also the days of Nehemiah, or just a little after them) the whole Jewish community in Jerusalem was being imperilled by this practice of inter-marriage with pagan women. Everybody was doing it. Nehemiah found himself in a situation where half the children in the city were speaking Philistine, or Ammonite or Moabite. They could not understand Hebrew or Aramaic, because their mothers did not speak it. What is more, many of the most prominent leaders in the community were involved.

That may very well be what Malachi is getting at when he says in verse 12, 'whoever he may be'. There was a real danger that the cultural attrition that these marriages were producing in the Jewish community would go unremedied, because the national leadership itself was hopelessly compromised by the practice.

The governor, Nehemiah, had to take some very draconian actions to remedy the situation; publicly rebuking very senior men, and insisting that Jews separate from their foreign wives. And it is important to realize that these words of Malachi are addressed to that same perilous and extreme historical situation. That is the first thing to note.

Malachi was an Old Testament prophet

The second is that there is something distinctive about the Old Testament period as far as inter-marriage is concerned. At this time, the whole plan of redemption hinged on the purity and survival of a particular nation. It was vital that when Christ came he should be born into a social context where people knew God's law, a place where people had read the prophets and were anticipating the Messiah the prophets had promised.

This was the very purpose of Israel in God's plan, that she should provide the arena in which the Saviour of the world would be born. But all that could be lost if Israel became dissolved in the cultural melting pot of the ancient world. That is why, 'theologically' if you like, God supports Nehemiah and Malachi in this very strong line against inter-marriage; because inter-marriage was perilous for the whole plan of redemption. The survival of the people of Israel as a culturally intact, pure people was essential to his cosmic purpose.

Inter-marriage in the New Testament

When we come to New Testament times, this negative appraisal of inter-marriage is still there, but it is far less strident. There are two reasons. The first is that the historical situation has changed and the second is that the theological situation has changed. The historical situation is different, because now there are many, many Christians who are legitimately and unavoidably married to non-Christians. Some of these were converted from Gentile homes and families. They were already married to pagans when they became Christians. There was no way they could avoid that situation. More than that, the social structure of the first century meant that marriages were often arranged by parents, so a young Christian may well find he had no choice but to marry a young pagan woman, because his parents insisted upon it. Such people simply could not be blamed for the marital partners they finished up with. The church was bound to have many such mixed marriages in it; the more successful its evangelism, the more it would be faced with this problem.

But not only has the historical situation changed in the New Testament; the theological situation has changed too. In the New Testament God's purpose is no longer dependent upon the survival of a particular ethnic group, with a particular cultural background. The church now comprises people of all nations and cultures. For this new covenant, which Jesus Christ has inaugurated, is no longer based on a genetic pedigree. It is based now on a spiritual affiliation – one generated not by physical birth, but by the birth of the Spirit. Thus it is that when Paul has to wrestle with this situation of mixed marriages in the New Testament, he treats it far less severely than Malachi does.

You do not find, for example, the apostles throwing people out of the church because they are married to non-Christians. Rather the contrary. In 1 Corinthians 7:12–16, Paul deals with some who, perhaps under the influence of Old Testament teaching, were saying: 'We should divorce our pagan partners.'

Paul's response is a negative one. 'No, that's not what you should do,' he says. 'In these New Testament days, there is no desecration of the church as a result of a mixed marriage as there was desecration of the temple in Malachi's day. Our situation is different. Rather, the unbelieving husband or wife is sanctified by the believing wife or husband. For the believer does not bring contamination into the church because at home he or she has an unbelieving partner. No; believers take a holy, sanctifying influence back into their homes from the church. That is how you must look at it,' says Paul.

This is very important, of course, for any of you involved in one way or another with a mixed marriage. Whether by choice or by an unavoidable divine providence, your spouse is not a Christian. I would not wish you, if that is your situation, to be unduly dismayed in consequence. In Malachi's day a pagan spouse represented a defilement of the sanctuary and a great peril to the destiny of God's people, but in the New Testament a pagan spouse is regarded as an opportunity for evangelism. Paul says, in 1 Corinthians 7, 'Think about it, maybe you will be the means of saving your unbelieving partner. Do not divorce him or her.' It is a view that Peter supports in his first letter. 'If your husband does not believe the word,' he says to the Christian woman, 'then go out of your way to be a good and faithful wife. Maybe he will be won over to the faith by the purity and reverence of your life' (cf. 1 Pet. 3:1–2).

If you are involved in a mixed marriage, that must be your unceasing hope and prayer. Do not treat your marriage as some kind of spiritual handicap that condemns you for ever to God's second best. It is not so. By the presence of the Holy Spirit in your life you bring a sanctifying influence into your family, which can only be for their good.

But – and it is a very big but – that does not mean that in the New Testament, the apostles encouraged mixed marriages in the church. They did not; in 2 Corinthians the apostle Paul also warns of the danger of being unequally yoked with unbelievers (2 Cor. 6:14). And it may very well be that marriage is one of those unequal yokes that he is talking about. Certainly, when in 1 Corinthians 7 he discusses a person who is free to choose her marital partner (as, in the ancient world, a widow was), he insists that the one she marries 'must belong to the Lord' (1 Cor. 7:39); that is, he must be a Christian.

So those of you who are single must not interpret the New Testament's more moderate attitude to mixed marriage, in comparison with Malachi's very tough line, as an invitation to contract marital relationships with non-Christians as if such things were innocuous. It is not so. The spiritual danger of mixed marriage is still there, because God's covenant is still there. The difference is that when you marry someone who is not a Christian, you are not imperilling the church, in the way that these people were imperilling Israel. But you are still imperilling your own spiritual well-being personally, for you are diminishing that covenant relationship with God which ought to come first in your life. You are breaking faith with him.

If you do not believe that a mixed marriage can do you spiritual harm, go and talk to people who are involved in mixed marriages. You will not find them telling you, 'Oh, it's OK! You go ahead. No problem.'

No; they will tell you it is hard. All kinds of conflicts of loyalty arise within a mixed marriage, which the Christian couple does not have to face. And there are temptations to spiritual backsliding which may well prove irresistible, and which, in far too many cases, do prove irresistible. Every pastor can tell you the sad tale of young men and women who seemed to show such potential for Christian service, but have finished up as casualties because their hormones got the better of them. They started by going out with non-Christians, because of course they wanted to 'witness' to them; they finished up by getting married to them.

Be sure of this, God is interested in whom you marry. Your vertical relationship with him demands that you make that choice wisely and prayerfully, for that relationship with him can be irreparably damaged by a foolish and rebellious choice. In that sense, Malachi's words here are just as relevant to you as a Christian as they were to those Jews. Do not marry the daughter of a foreign god. To do so deliberately is to court disaster; it is to break faith with the God who loves you and has called you to be his own. It is to break faith with Jesus, every bit as much as these Jews were breaking faith with Jehovah. And that brings us to the second kind of unfaithfulness which was being exhibited in Israel.

Unfaithfulness in marriage

In Britain every day of the week, thousands of marriages break up, many in savage pain. One partner walks out on the other, usually into the arms of someone else: 'I know you will understand,' says the farewell note on the mantelpiece. But the truth in many cases is, of course, that they do not understand. Because when someone you love leaves you for someone else, it hurts. Few things in this world hurt more.

It is popular today to treat that old commandment 'You shall not commit adultery' as the vestigial remains of an outdated moral straitjacket. We are in the post-permissive society. Extra-marital sex is not even naughty any more, it's normal. To suggest sexual continence as a possible solution to the Aids problem is to invite ridicule. It is almost as bad as recommending the reintroduction of chastity belts. Opinion polls prove conclusively that the majority of men and women today expect to experience sexual intercourse with several partners during their lifetime.

Indeed, some sociologists argue that we are technically no longer a monogamous society. It would be closer to the truth to describe the marital situation in the western world today as serial polygamy – the convention of having only one sexual partner at a time. As someone has put it, 'It is not so much a case of "Marry in haste and repent at leisure" as "Marry in haste and repeat at leisure".'

Something very similar was happening in Malachi's day (2:13–14). As we said on our first morning, these Jews were treating divorce as casually as they would trading in an old car. A man looked at the wife he had married some years ago, and noticed that she was beginning to sag a bit in the suspension and that her bodywork was deteriorating. 'It's time for a new model,' he thought to himself. And that was it; no thought that marriage was a covenant, a promise. No thought that this was a one-flesh union, sealed by God himself. 'Everybody is doing it. We will remain good friends, won't we? I have just discovered, after fifteen years of married life, that we are incompatible. That's all.'

As far as Malachi was concerned, all the excuses collapsed when confronted with one single sentence in verse 16: '"I hate divorce," says the LORD God of Israel.' In my book, God says, divorce is as serious a crime as murder: I hate it as implacably as I hate a man 'covering himself with violence'. To tolerate divorce in the complacent way you people have been doing, therefore, is just one more symptom of your spiritual half-heartedness, one more proof of your faith-lessness.

Now once again we need to make some careful qualifications, if we are to avoid causing unnecessary hurt. Let me give you three.

1. Divorce is not impossible

Malachi knew perfectly well that divorce was actually permitted in God's law, and that Moses made provision for it in Deuteronomy 24:1–4. You may ask, why did God do such a thing if he hated divorce so much? The answer is given to us from Jesus' own lips. He said, 'Moses permitted you to divorce your wives because your hearts were hard' (Mt. 19:8). Sometimes God has to make concessions to the fallenness of human nature. We cannot keep his law perfectly, and so it is occasionally a lesser evil to permit his moral law to be broken in, as it were, a regulated fashion that minimizes the consequent damage, than to enforce that law rigidly and uncompromisingly. That is what Moses' divorce law was all about, says Jesus. It was a concession to our hard hearts, but it was not what God really wanted. He knew that keeping a couple together who were determined to break up was just unrealistic; it would do more harm than good. So the law had to make some provision for divorce as an inevitable fact of life in a fallen world. In that sense, divorce is possible – but that does not mean God likes it. On the contrary, he hates it.

2. In some divorces there may be an innocent partner

Malachi does not deny it. Indeed he suggests that the majority of divorces happening in his day did involve such an innocent partner. The abandoned wife was being deserted by her husband for no good reason at all, he said. She was an innocent partner in the affair.

No doubt there are two sides to every story. But the Bible does make a clear distinction between the sort of behaviour which undermines marital happiness and the sort of behaviour which breaks a marital bond. Jesus, in his teaching on divorce in the gospels, seems quite clearly to recognize for instance that adultery constitutes grounds for divorce, and that a husband or wife separating from a partner in such circumstances is not sinning (see Mt. 5:31–32). Similarly in 1 Corinthians 7 Paul seems to regard desertion by an unbelieving partner as grounds for divorce (see 1 Cor. 7:15). These are areas of controversy, as I am sure many of you are aware. Not all evangelical interpreters would endorse all that I have just said. But Malachi is certainly not denying that in many divorces there is an innocent partner, who experiences the pain of the break-up without deserving it.

3. Divorce is not an unforgivable sin

Malachi is not saying here that a divorcee, even if he or she is partially or totally responsible for the marital breakdown, has committed an unforgivable sin. God hates all sins. But no sin is unforgivable, except the repudiation of the work of God the Holy Spirit in our lives. Forgiveness is always available, as we were seeing last night in Psalm 51. In fact, God has a wonderful way of repairing lives shattered by divorce, and every pastor can tell you stories of that. But that is not to say that there are no painful consequences in our lives as a result of divorce. Divorce leaves debris – hurt feelings which may take years to heal.

Often, of course, there are children to be considered. Verse 15 is unfortunately almost untranslatable from the Hebrew. But Malachi seems to be acknowledging in it that one of God's purposes in marriage is godly offspring. That is one reason he is so concerned about the sanctity of marriage; because the emotional and moral stability of children hinges on their experience of the faithfulness of the marriage bond. If they do not observe their mother and father being faithful to one another, they will not learn how important it is to be faithful in human relationships generally.

It should cause no surprise that the moral behaviour of children and young people gives such cause for concern in our society today. Any society in which almost every other marriage ends in divorce is going to be a society saturated with children who have suffered emotional and moral damage to their lives. It is an inevitable consequence of our shabby example of love. The murder of a little child by two ten-year-olds, the rape of a teacher by a teenage pupil – of course such stories horrify the nation; but it is no good beating our breasts and saying 'Bring back the cane' or 'Rebuild the Borstals', as if that were going to change the situation. We are beginning to experience the moral fallout of our statistics of broken marriages. And we have not seen a fraction of it yet.

Nevertheless, our situation is not without hope. Christ can repair lives which divorce has blown apart – the lives of the divorcees themselves, and the lives of the children. He can work in that situation of brokenness and evil and turn it to his good, by his over-ruling purpose and grace. I am sure that some of you here can testify to such a miracle. So we do not need to despair in a situation of divorce, as though we have committed an unforgivable sin that can never be resolved.

God hates divorce

Nevertheless, having said all these things – that divorce is possible; that there is an innocent partner sometimes; and that divorce can be forgiven – it would be irresponsible of me this morning if I did not draw your attention to the unequivocal language with which God expresses his outrage concerning divorce.

'I hate it,' he says.

Why? Because of the hurt it causes to the partner? Of course. Because of the damage it does to the children? Of course. But most of all, he hates it because it is one more example of broken faith, of promises not kept. Relationships depend on promises; and to treat divorce as casually as these Jews were treating it was to invite a collapse in relationships and therefore in society generally. There could be no deep and satisfying commitment of one person to another in a world that did not understand the importance of faithfulness. And of course it is just such a society that we are generating for ourselves.

Listen to these words from Christopher Lasch, in his book *The Culture of Narcissism*:

> Our society . . . has made deep and lasting friendships, love affairs, and marriages increasingly difficult to achieve. As social life has become more and more warlike and barbaric, personal relationships . . . take on the character of combat. Some of the new therapies dignify this combat as 'assertiveness'. Others celebrate impermanent attachments under such formulas as 'open marriage'. Thus they intensify the disease they pretend to cure.

People in our world today are lonely, and getting lonelier – because, as Hosea says, there is no faithfulness, no love, in the land (Ho. 4:1). People cannot trust each other any more, because they will not keep a promise.

Erich Fromm, in his books *The Art of Loving* and *The Sane Society*, blames it all on the economic system. Capitalism, he says, reduces all relationships to self-interest. It makes real love impossible by its cultivation of individualism. Men and women do not really love one another any more in a capitalist society; they just use each other for the fulfilment of their individualistic needs, rather as a car owner uses a mechanic to service his car.

Other sociologists draw attention to the effects of eroticization of modern society by the media. Forty years ago the publication of D. H. Lawrence's novel *Lady Chatterley's Lover* was sufficient to scandalize the nation and bring about a court action. Now we have soft-porn videos, thinly disguised as sex-education courses, on sale in Woolworth's. We have girlie magazines, that would once have been found only in some curtained Soho dive, on public display in the High Street newsagent's. And our advertisers seem incapable of marketing even so ordinary a consumable as a bar of chocolate without turning it into an object of phallic fantasy. Expectations of sexual athleticism in one's partner, and of sexual ecstasy in oneself, have risen to extraordinary heights. I suspect that not since the closing days of the Roman Empire has the general level of sexual arousal in a society been quite so high as it is in ours. And in such an environment, it is not surprising if the boundary between love and lust gets rather blurred.

So is capitalism to blame for the shallow quality of our relationships? Or is it the exploitation of sex by the media? I do not deny that those things play a part, but I suggest to you that it is Malachi who has the deepest insight: at the root of our problem is unfaithfulness, an unwillingness on our part to be bound to anybody by promise.

In the 1980s a group of sociologists at the University of Berkeley in California carried out a very interesting study which was published as *Habits of the Heart*. One of the most important questions they addressed concerned contemporary attitudes to feelings. They found that people holding traditional ideas took the view that feelings should always take second place to duty. So they placed a higher value on virtues such as self-control, self-denial, self-discipline and self-sacrifice. Marital love was seen as fundamentally a commitment of the will, which one ought to honour irrespective of one's personal feelings about it, whether good or bad.

But these researchers discovered an interesting thing; that the traditional view was rapidly being displaced in the West by another attitude, which they characterized as the 'therapeutic attitude'. On this view, feelings take priority over everything else. The important thing is not what restrains the expression of the self, but rather what liberates it. Honesty and openness are what count, not self-discipline or self-denial or self-control. Self-realization, self-fulfilment, self-acceptance, self-actualization – these are the buzz-words of the therapeutic attitude. 'The spontaneous sharing of feelings between authentic expressive individuals' – this is the therapeutic definition of love.

Long-term commitment does not necessarily feature at all in such relationships. According to the therapeutic attitude, if my emotional needs are not being met by my partner I am entitled to ditch them. The therapeutic attitude denies all forms of social obligation and replaces them simply by the ideal of open and honest communication between people. The only thing therapeutically liberated lovers owe their partners is to share their feelings fully with them. Emotional independence and self-sufficiency are the goal; and a personal relationship is seen merely as a device for achieving those essential individualistic ends.

Now I am not saying that the therapeutic attitude is all bad. Undoubtedly, it does do some a great service by helping them to get in touch with their own wants and needs, and emancipating them from the artificial constraints of a social role which is inappropriate to them. But it has to be said that, carried to its extreme, this sort of attitude is desperately corrosive of the marriage bond, because it destroys faithfulness. As far as the Bible is concerned, the key thing that makes us human is our ability to form relationships, and there can be no relationships, either with God or with our neighbour, unless we are able to be faithful to one another.

Love is not just a feeling intended for our private

enjoyment. It is a covenant that binds two people together. Love is not a passion; it is a promise. You know the reason most people shy away from marriage today, why they do not even bother getting married, let alone divorced? They are scared of it. Those vows are just too permanent. Promise to love somebody for better for worse, for richer for poorer, till death us do part? 'Why,' says our twentieth-century Romeo or Juliet incredulously, 'you cannot possibly expect me to make an unconditional commitment like that. If they cannot do it in the Royal Family, how can they expect me to do it? Life-long promises are out of place where your feelings are concerned. Nobody knows how I am going to feel about someone else in ten hours' time, let alone ten years. There's no controlling Cupid. He is a capricious and arbitrary imp. He makes no promises, so how can I?'

'You fall in love, you fall out of love,' asserts our Romeo. 'It is sentimental measles; you catch it, you recover from it. Certainly you cannot rely on it. Those who gamble on love lasting for ever are backing a horse that regularly falls before the first fence. Where relationships are concerned, the wise keep their options open. Do not put all your eggs in one basket. Enjoy it while it lasts!'

But the Bible insists that that is all rubbish. There is a stronger kind of love than that, a dependable love. How do we know it? We know it because God has shown it to us. He is a faithful, covenant God. 'I have loved you,' he tells them. There is a cross on a hill, where the blood of God was shed to make a covenant with us. There is his promise written indelibly and by his own hand for the universe to see. 'I love you and I do not intend to stop loving you. I will give my very self for you.'

That is the kind of love he expects us to emulate. Not a passing whim, born of romantic sentiment or sexual lust, but a strong, endurable covenant. That's what God means by love. Not a feeling, but a promise.

So, says Malachi, guard yourself in your spirit and do not break faith. Watch those wandering eyes, control those illicit fantasies. Settle it in your heart, he says, that you will not break faith: not with your marital partner, not with your God. 'Be faithful, even to the point of death,' God says, 'and I will give you the crown of life' (Rev. 2:10).

4

Cynicism

Malachi 2:17 – 4:6

When I was a young Christian, the question of rewards gave me a lot of trouble. It seemed rather discreditable to me that God should offer Christians incentives. It appeared to pander to the acquisitive spirit. The essence of the Christian ethic is unselfishness and altruism, so surely if people are going to serve God, let it be because he is worthy of it, not because they think they are going to get something out of it.

I was a great admirer in those days of a hymn by Francis Xavier which we used to sing at school:

> My God, I love thee, not because
>   I hope for heaven thereby;
> Nor yet because who love thee not
>   Are lost eternally.
>
> Not with the hope of gaining aught,
>   Not seeking a reward . . .
> Solely because thou art my God
>   And my most loving King.

Noble words, and bang on target, I thought. If God be God, then the matter of following him was an utterly thankless task with no hint of personal advantage. Integrity surely demands I honour him. Faith is not a bargain I strike on the basis of some calculated profit margin. Faith is my unconditional surrender to the irresistible claim of God's truth upon my conscience.

Or so I thought in those early days. And in many respects I still think like that. I do not approve, for instance, of evangelists who try to gain converts by offering inducements; by promising healing to the sick or prosperity to the poor, rice to the hungry – or visas to the refugees, come to that. Such tactics are simply bribery, and those who respond to such appeals are likely to have no more true faith in them than a mercenary has true patriotism. No, the highest motive for becoming a Christian is that we want God in our lives, not the blessings that God may give us. Francis Xavier's hymn is a masterly expression of that sentiment.

But as the years go by I have to confess that my youthful idealism has been moderated somewhat on this matter. I have discovered just how difficult it is to sustain the Christian faith in this broken and unhappy world in which we live. There are an awful lot of things around that contradict a breezy confidence in God, are there not? There are crime, war, natural disaster and sickness; tragedies of a dozen kinds are reported in our newspapers daily.

And such things quite clearly happen in a way that makes no distinction between good people and bad people, between Christians and non-Christians. Adversity is un-discriminating and arbitrary – at least, so it seems. The innocent suffer just as much as the guilty; indeed, some-times, the innocent seem to suffer far more than the guilty. The guilty, precisely because they are unscrupulous and self-centred, all too often get away with murder. Do you know this little rhyme?

> The rain it raineth on the just
>   And also on the unjust fella:
> But chiefly on the just, because
>   The unjust steals the just's umbrella.
>   (Baron Bowen Charles, 1835–94)

It is precisely this unfairness which Malachi's compatriots are complaining about in this final section of his prophecy. 'What is the point of religion?' they ask. 'It's all very well for preachers like Malachi to pontificate about a God of righteousness, but he has created an unjust world.'

It is not hard to feel some sympathy for such complaints. I think we have to acknowledge that the most serious objection that could be raised against the theistic faith of the Bible is the problem of evil in the world. Other religions can adopt the dualistic solution. They can say,

'Well, there are equal and opposite powers of good and evil in the world, locked in a never-ending struggle. All the good things that happen derive from the good force, from God, and all the bad things that happen derive from the bad force – that is, the devil.'

It is a very convenient theory. But unfortunately, the Bible cannot endorse it. No, it says; God is an absolute sovereign in his universe. Nothing happens outside his control. The devil is no more than a malevolent rebel spirit, a creation of God, and far inferior to him in both power and knowledge. The book of Job tells us that he has no ability to harm human beings, except as God gives him permission to do so.

In many respects this doctrine of divine omnipotence is very comforting, but it inevitably invites the question: 'Well then, why does this sovereign God give the devil so much rope?' Again, other religions can take refuge in monism. The monistic solution to the problem of evil says that God is in everything, both 'good' and 'evil'. All distinctions of that sort in the universe are really illusory. For there is no evil except as we choose to call it so. Christian Science comes very close to this when it tells us that pain is all in the mind.

> There was a faith healer of Deal
> Who said, 'Though I know pain ain't real,
>   When I sit on a pin
>   And it punctures my skin,
> I dislike what I fancy I feel.'

Convenient as the monistic solution to the problem of evil is, once again the Bible cannot accept it. It insists that God is good, that he loves what is just and right, that he stands over against all forms of evil, that he does not enjoy the pain or suffering of his creation in any way; and that is why goodness really matters, because it matters to him.

But once again, reassuring though a doctrine of divine righteousness is, it invites the objection: 'If God hates all this evil and suffering so much, why does he go on tolerating it?' So the Christian feels exceptionally vulnerable on this issue of evil. The Bible forces us to tread a difficult path between dualism and monism, to believe in an almighty God who for some reason is allowing things to go on in his universe to which he is thoroughly opposed. It is not difficult for atheists to ridicule such an idea. Bertrand Russell said, 'I can imagine a sardonic demon making us for his amusement, but I cannot attribute to a God who is almighty and bene-volent the appalling weight of misery and degradation which has so marred the history of mankind.'

Malachi's compatriots were basically expressing the same scepticism; with less erudition, and in a rather sulkier tone perhaps, but it was essentially the same point they were making.

'All who do evil are good in the eyes of the LORD, and he is pleased with them' (2:17).

'Look,' they were saying, 'there is brother Eliezer over there; everyone knows he has a mistress on the other side of town. It does not seem to diminish his business profits, does it? And then there's Jonah the rent collector over there, crooked as they come. He always wears a very nice suit, you notice. As for caring for the weak in society, the widow, the orphan and the refugee – forget it. That's a mug's game. Don't you know we are in the middle of a recession, Mala-chi? Look after number one, that's the only sensible policy. If God is so concerned that we Jews should keep his law, how come all the pagans have got all the money?

'No, religion is just a big confidence trick. What is the point of performing all those religious rituals, praying all those prayers? It's the proud and the oppressors who get on in life, not the meek and the lowly ones. People can defy God, even curse him to his face, and nothing happens to them.'

'It is futile to serve God. What did we gain by carrying out his requirements and going about like mourners before the LORD Almighty? But now we call the arrogant blessed. Cer-tainly the evildoers prosper, and even those who challenge God escape' (3:14–15).

To Malachi this is undoubtedly the most difficult aspect of his people's spiritual declension with which he has to deal. Their apathy in worship and their infidelity in personal relationships he can counter by appeal or by admonition. But at the root of this aspect of their spiritual half-heartedness lies not just laziness, indiscipline or sensuality, but a profound doubt about the goodness and dependability of God.

And that is what makes the situation so serious and dangerous. Kenneth Clark in his great book *Civilisation* writes: 'We can destroy ourselves by cynicism, just as much as by bombs.' He is absolutely right about that, of course, for the cynic has lost confidence in values. The cynic says that it is an unjust world, that virtue is triumphant only in theatricals and that once a people has surrendered to that kind of radical pessimism and cynicism, then moral anarchy, social decadence and pandemic despair are the inevitable consequences. That sort of cynicism is just as devastating as war, and there are plenty of civilizations that have fallen prey to its self-destructiveness.

The reply to cynicism

How was Malachi to address such a pernicious cancer in his society? There is really only one way. It is the Bible doctrine of rewards. Malachi cannot deny the negative and demoralizing aspects of human experience, of which these cynics complain; but he *can* insist that it is only one side of the story, a passing hiccup, an ephemeral blip in the moral order of the universe. 'No,' he says, 'it is *worth* serving God. Those who do not serve him will be losers in the long run. It is worth pursuing goodness. Those who do not do so will pay a price for their wickedness, in the last analysis.'

That hymn of Francis Xavier is all very fine and noble – but it is also naive and sentimental. 'My God, I love thee, not because I hope for heaven thereby' – but if there is no heaven to hope for, how on earth can any love for God survive in this sin-sick world in which we live?

The whole point about the Christian faith is that it offers the final vindication of the goodness of God. No matter how dispassionate our quest for religious truth may be, no matter how high-minded our spiritual aspiration may be, there is no way a faith like that can be rationally sustained in the face of present evil without a doctrine of rewards. That is why there is no embarrassment in Malachi's recourse to that doctrine here in order to counter the embittered cynicism of his society. Reward is not some bait on his evangelistic hook by which he is unscrupulously enticing the people of his day to believe. Rewards, for Malachi, are the necessary consequence of that victory over sin which God must win if there is to be any gospel for the evangelist to proclaim at all.

If we do not believe in rewards, how can we any longer believe in God? It is not because the Bible loses its veracity in the absence of rewards for goodness; but because, if there are no rewards for goodness, the victory of God about which the Bible speaks loses its credibility.

Some of us perhaps have been moved by our studies in Malachi. We have made resolutions to be less apathetic, less indifferent, more committed. And it is a good thing to make such resolutions; but I tell you this – they will not endure a month, perhaps not even a week, battling in the gale of adversity, fighting the tide of rampant wickedness in our world unless we are convinced it's all going to be worth it – unless we are convinced that God must win, and that because he must win, we shall be winners too. How does Paul put it? 'We share in his sufferings in order that we may also share in his glory' (Rom. 8:17).

The rewards of commitment

What are these rewards for whole-heartedness, to which Malachi draws our attention in these closing chapters? There are two kinds. In 3:6–12, Malachi teaches us that there is a reward for godliness in this world, in the here and now. But in 3:1–5 and in 3:13 – 4:6 he points also to rewards that lie in the future, that belong to the last day.

Present rewards

'"Bring the whole tithe into the storehouse, that there may be food in my house. Test me in this," says the LORD Almighty, "and see if I will not throw open the floodgates of heaven and pour out so much blessing that you will not have room enough for it"' (3:10).

73

It is clear from 3:10–12 that one of the ways in which the half-heartedness of the Jewish community was revealing itself in Malachi's day was the lack of funds in the temple treasury. The people simply were not giving generously to God. It is no surprise: people who are too mean to give a good animal sacrifice are hardly likely to put their hands in their pockets for cash any more readily. But the verdict which Malachi passes on this parsimony may come as something of a shock, nevertheless.

'Will a man rob God? Yet you rob me . . . You are under a curse – the whole nation of you – because you are robbing me' (3:8–9).

Malachi's point here is that in the Old Testament, people were required by law to donate one tenth of their annual income to the temple. It belonged to God by right according to the law. So to withhold it, said Malachi, is nothing short of larceny. 'Is it any wonder, then,' he says, 'that there is an economic recession? Is it any wonder there is no food in the shops, that Israel's reputation internationally is at an all-time low? Why on earth should God bless a den of thieves? It is not as though he deserves such treatment.'

All through history, says Malachi (verse 7), Israel has been abandoning the Lord, kicking him in the teeth, refusing to do things his way; when all through history God has been faithful to his covenant, he has never given up on us. 'That,' says Malachi, 'is why we are here in Jerusalem today. "I, the LORD, do not change" – that is why you descendants of Jacob are not destroyed.

'If he has denied us economic affluence, then, he is only fulfilling the promise he made to Moses. He told us in his law that if we as a nation ignore his moral rules, we will forfeit his economic blessings. But he also told us that if we repented of our sins, he would restore our prosperity' (cf. 3:6–7).

'Isn't it about time', asks Malachi, 'that we broke this habitual cycle of apostasy? God invites us to do so. He never stops wanting us to do so.

'Return to me,' he says, 'and I will return to you.' The

promises of the covenant and the prosperity that goes with them are there waiting to be claimed by you. And', says Malachi, 'there is a very simple way to prove it.'

'If you want to return, do so in your tithes and offerings,' says Malachi. 'Put my covenant promise to the test,' says God; 'see if it is not true that those who honour me, I will honour. The measure you give will be the measure you get. See if it is not true that I will open the floodgates of heaven and pour out so much blessing on you that you will not have enough room for it. There is a reward for a whole-hearted commitment to me in the here and now. And once I see the sign of your restored whole-heartedness in those tithes and offerings, you shall receive it. You have only yourselves to blame for your current economic austerities. You will never discover the prosperity God wants you to enjoy while your mean fists are grasping your wallets so tightly whenever you come to church' (cf. 3:10–12).

It is a very bold challenge, is it not? How do you think we should apply that to our contemporary situation? Is Malachi proposing a kind of prosperity doctrine? Give to God and he will give back to you, just like that? There are plenty of preachers, of course, who have interpreted this text in exactly that way. There are countless churches that invite you, not to give, but to 'invest' in their work; the implication is that you will get a return with interest. And who has not heard the testimony of those Christian business people who assure us that it was only when they started to tithe that, miraculously, commercial success began to be their lot?

But I want to suggest that it would be a mistake to read this passage as an endorsement of that kind of prosperity teaching.

The promise is to a nation

First, we see that Malachi's words are directed to the nation as a whole, not to individuals; because, of course, the law of Deuteronomy was addressed to society generally. That law promises economic blessing to the people that obey God, but the Bible is far more chary about individualizing those material rewards. Scripture gives us for example the story of

Job, a good man who obeyed God's law completely and yet who experienced poverty rather than wealth.

Let us be as realistic about this as the Bible is. For every Christian business person who testifies to the prosperity God has brought his or her way, there is another silent in the pew, broken by bankruptcy. I am not saying that God does not bless us as individuals materially. Undoubtedly he does, but there is no mechanical and inevitable link between the amount of money I put in the offering bag on Sunday and the amount of money in my pay packet on Friday. The blessings of which Malachi speaks here concern the macro-economy of the national, rather than the micro-economy of the individual.

Malachi is an Old Testament prophet

Secondly, just as in the case of inter-marriage which we examined yesterday, the Old Testament location of Malachi's words makes a vital difference. In his day, the people of God were a political entity and the temple of God was a national institution. But in New Testament days the church is an international community and the temple has been replaced by the spiritual solidarity of the body of Christ. It follows then that the blessings and rewards of Christian faithfulness of which the New Testament speaks tend to be spiritual rather than material, eternal rather than temporal.

Now, it is true that there are compensations promised by Jesus to offset the cost of discipleship. But there is nothing in the gospel to suggest that the Christian disciple should expect to be wealthy. In fact the reverse is true. Sell what you have and give to the poor, and you will have treasure in *heaven* – that was Jesus' emphasis. He certainly said, 'Seek first God's kingdom and your material welfare will be taken care of' (*cf.* Mt. 6:33), but he was talking about food and clothing, not Aston Martins and caviar.

So how should we apply Malachi's challenge to his people, to ourselves and to our present day? Let me offer just a few hints.

I think that first of all, a careful application of his words can be rightly directed to *our nation*. Does this mean that the

Archbishop of Canterbury should be recommending to the Chancellor of the Exchequer that the way out of the recession is to put 10p on income tax, and devote the resulting revenue to the refurbishment of the Church of England and the remuneration of its clergy? At the risk of disappointing my Anglican friends, I have to say no, I have no confidence in such a policy at all. But I think the passage can be applied in this sense – that we, the body of Christ, as a prophetic community in our nation, should be as courageous as Malachi is in drawing the connection between economic decay and moral ills in our community.

Secondly, I think this is a passage that can be rightly applied within *our churches*. Does this mean that the pastor should insist upon 10% tithing of income as a requirement of church membership? No. That would be a legalistic measure, out of place in the New Testament church. But the principle of giving to God's work regularly a proportion of our wealth, prayerfully determined, as Paul said in 2 Corinthians 8:11, in keeping with our income, seems to me a principle the New Testament fully endorses. We should be teaching our churches that if our people give in that kind of committed way, then we, as the community of God's people, will find he opens the floodgates of heaven and pours out blessing upon us. Paul says something with which Malachi would have agreed, when he says, 'Whoever sows sparingly will also reap sparingly, and whoever sows generously will also reap generously' (2 Cor. 9:6).

And I think there is a sense in which these words do rightly apply to *us as individuals* too. Do you want to return to God? Have you been touched by God's word, and are you seeking some way of responding to the challenge, to be 100% for God in future? Well, Malachi here is suggesting one way you can do it: a simple, practical, concrete way of consolidating that resolution. Christian discipleship begins in the head, as we understand what God's word demands of us. Christian discipleship proceeds to the heart, where we respond willingly to the demands God places upon us. And between the head and the heart, Christian discipleship passes through the pocket. If it does not, it is not real; that is what Malachi is saying. If you really mean that you want to return to God, the offering basket will be fuller next Sunday.

Put God to the test, then. There are rewards for the whole-hearted believer. Giving is good for you, not an onerous duty. It is a joyful privilege; it is a pathway to blessing. Malachi is convinced you cannot out-give God, but he does invite you to try.

Future rewards

There are present rewards for the faithful believer, then, but there are even greater rewards yet to come!

> 'See, I will send my messenger, who will prepare
> the way before me. Then suddenly the LORD you
> are seeking will come to his temple; the messenger
> of the covenant, whom you desire, will come,' says
> the LORD Almighty (3:1).

One of the most characteristic features of our contemporary world is its loss of hope. It was Woody Allen who made the remark that the future is not what it used to be. He was right. Optimism about the destiny of the human race has collapsed in our century. That vision of Utopia, the fire and political idealism of an earlier generation, lie wrecked under the carnage of a dozen bloody wars and revolutions. All those predictions of technological progress that motivated the scientific enterprise have been shrouded in the mushroom cloud of Hiroshima and the pollution of Chernobyl.

A few still cling to the old Utopian dreams of a man-made paradise on earth. They talk of a New Age now, the Age of Aquarius. But the vast majority of thinking people today are no longer wearing rose-tinted spectacles of such a discredited humanism.

Kenneth Clark, in the book *Civilisation* which I mentioned earlier, says this: 'Confident articles on the future are, to my mind, the most disreputable of all public utterances.' And as the millennial year of AD 2000 approaches, I suspect that global insecurity will become more and more acute.

Malachi's compatriots seem to have been interested in the idea of a Utopian new age too. They loved to speculate about the prophetic predictions of a coming Day of the Lord when God would intervene miraculously and establish Jerusalem as the capital of the entire world. That dream had fired many of them as they returned to Jerusalem from Babylon. They were like some Zionists today; they believed the kingdom of God was imminent. They had come home to get Jerusalem ready for the Messiah, for the Lord's coming.

But Malachi has some words of caution to offer them in respect of that eschatological enthusiasm of theirs.

God will come in judgment

> But who can endure the day of his coming? Who can stand when he appears? For he will be like a refiner's fire or a launderer's soap. He will sit as a refiner and purifier of silver; he will purify the Levites and refine them like gold and silver. Then the LORD will have men who will bring offerings in righteousness, and the offerings of Judah and Jerusalem will be acceptable to the LORD, as in days gone by, as in former years (3:2–4).

The Day of the Lord is certainly going to arrive, he says. God will come. In fact shortly he will send the prophetic forerunner to prepare for that day, the one he calls in 3:1 'my messenger', and in 4:5 'the prophet Elijah', whom 'I will send . . . before that great and dreadful day of the LORD comes'. But are you really sure you want that Day to come? For let's face it, says Malachi, you are a half-hearted people. Your public worship is apathetic, your lives are selfish and sinful, and your attitudes are just thoroughly cynical. There is no way that coming day is going to be a pleasant experience for people like you. 'Who can endure the day of his coming? Who can stand when he appears?' (3:2).

For it is going to be a day of judgment, a *refining* judgment, first of all purging the clergy of their compromise up there in the temple. 'He will be like a refiner's fire or a launderer's soap. He will sit as a refiner and purifier of silver' (3:2–3). Whom is he going to purify? Not the pagans, not even the people in the pew – the Levites. 'He . . . will refine them like gold and silver. Then the LORD will have men who will bring offerings in righteousness, and the offerings of Judah and Jerusalem will be acceptable to the LORD, as in the days gone by, as in former years' (3:3–4).

It is going to be a retributory judgment too, punishing a sinful, morally degenerate society.

'So I will come near to you for judgment. I will be quick to testify against sorcerors, adulterers and perjurers, against those who defraud labourers of their wages, who oppress the widows and the fatherless, and deprive aliens of justice, but do not fear me,' says the LORD Almighty' (3:5).

There are countless sins that bear no penalty in our statute book. But God will execute judgment against them all. The sorcerers, the perjurers, the adulterers, the oppressers – God will execute judgment against them all.

But most significant of all, for this cynical audience of Malachi's, it is going to be a *discriminating* judgment. The books are going to be opened, and the real people of God are going to be revealed. All lives will be assessed, and then it will be seen who has 'feared the LORD and honoured his name' (3:16).

'You will again see the distinction between the righteous and the wicked, between those who serve God and those who do not' (3:18).

'"Surely the day is coming; it will burn like a furnace. All the arrogant and every evildoer will be stubble, and that day that is coming will set them on fire," says the LORD Almighty. "Not a root or a branch will be left to them"' (4:1).

I do not like the idea of hell any more than you do. But, you see, *unless Malachi can speak of such a final judgment, the cynics are right*. Unless God imposes some ultimate sanction against the wickedness of the human race, his righteousness is a farce. Hell is not an embarrassment to heaven. God is glorified in judgment. For in judgment, he affirms his righteousness over against everything that denies it. And heaven is glad about that.

God will bring his reward with him

But not only will the wicked perish; there is a positive side to this Day of the Lord too. Those who fear the Lord and honour him ' "will be mine," says the LORD Almighty, "in the day when I make up my treasured possession. I will spare them, just as in compassion a man spares his son who serves him" ' (3:17).

'For you who revere my name, the sun of righteousness will rise with healing in its wings' (4:2).

All the darkness which clouds our faith and makes it hard going to believe in God at the moment is going to be dispelled when the sun of his justice finally sends those clouds scudding away. And then there will be no more suffering and pain for the righteous, only healing and mercy.

'You will go out and leap like calves released from the stall' (4:2).

Have you ever seen an animal released after being confined and frustrated by its cramped environment? It gambols all over the field in its new-found freedom. And in the same way, says Malachi, the true people of God who are struggling right in the frustrating confinement of this sin-sick world will find liberation. As Paul puts it, 'We ourselves, who have the firstfruits of the Spirit, groan inwardly as we wait eagerly for our adoption as sons, the redemption of our bodies' (Rom. 8:23). That groaning is not going to last for ever. The day of emancipation is coming, says Malachi; a day which will make all the suffering we have had to endure pale into insignificance by the radiance of its glory.

And when that day comes, ' "you will trample down the wicked; they will be ashes under the soles of your feet on the day when I do these things," says the LORD Almighty' (4:3).

No, heaven is not embarrassed by hell, and you and I will not be either. It will not spoil heaven for us to know that God has judged the wicked. We will understand that it is the only way that heaven can remain heaven.

Recapturing the dream

I ask you: can you survive in this world of ours without a hope like that?

There is so much cynicism today. A young American student at Cambridge who expressed it to me in words I have never forgotten. He said, 'We Americans used to trust the generals, but Vietnam changed all that. We used to trust the politicians, then Watergate changed all that. We used to trust the scientists, but Three Mile Island changed all that. We used to trust the economists, but recession changed all that. Now we know there is no-one to trust.'

He predicted, 'The l990s will be years of cynicism.' And so they have proved. The optimism of the past seems almost laughable. Experience has revealed it to be a fantasy of infantile human political imagination, as far removed from reality as Disneyland is from Hiroshima. And, I have to say, that disillusionment is most tragic. That does not mean that I grieve because the intoxicated expectations of the early socialists and the early humanists have been sobered by a few bucketfuls of cold political reality. I do not mourn that; it was very necessary. Nor does it sadden me that people are becoming more wary of technological advance. Scientific hubris is dangerous. As long as we do not plunge back into medieval superstition or Luddite paranoia, a little more ecological sensitivity and caution will be all to the good in our use of scientific discoveries.

No, what worries me is that mankind in the West has lost its dream.

We have lost the hope, the vision that gives meaning to our existence. It is not enough that we human beings should just survive; we need hope and a purpose. Without some incentive like that we languish into apathy – yes, and cynicism; and ultimately into despair. Take away everything that people have to live for, and they put a bullet through their brains. And we can see the signs of that suicidal apathy, cynicism and despair all around us in our contemporary society. People are shutting the future out of their minds in myopic self-indulgence. 'Let us eat, drink and be merry, for tomorrow – who knows? Enjoy yourself while you have a chance.' This is a world that has lost its hope.

Such a world is doomed. Slowly but surely, such pessimism tears the guts out of a culture. People have nothing to work for, nothing to save for, nothing to live for beyond the immediate satisfaction of their desires. That, it seems to me, is exactly why the West is finding it so hard to advance economically right now. High interest rates are a consequence of the desire for instant gratification. You have to penalize people for consuming, in order to stop them. But it does not matter how high a penalty you impose on consumption, a hopeless generation will go on buying to comfort itself for its lack of future.

Where is our society to turn for hope, in days like ours when secular dreams have lost their credibility? Christians have an answer. Indeed we should be more conspicuous on this ground than perhaps on any other – not just because we maintain habits of religious worship in a secular age, or just because we maintain standards of moral behaviour in a permissive age.

At the turn of the twenty-first century, the most obvious thing about Christians may be that we still have hope, that we have not surrendered to cynicism, that we still believe in the victory of goodness, that we are still looking forward to the future.

Why are we able to do that? Because the messenger of the covenant has come just as Malachi said he would, with John the Baptist as his prophetic forerunner. And now he stands at God's right hand, clothed in victory.

Dr David Cook tells a lovely story of an Oxford undergraduate who, in his final year, somewhere around June or July, wrote a letter to his parents.

> Dear Mum and Dad,
>
>   I know you haven't heard much from me in recent months, but the fact is this. A few weeks back, there was a fire in the flat and I lost all my possessions. In fact I only escaped with my life by jumping out of a second-floor window. In the process of doing so I broke my leg, so I finished up in hospital. Fortunately, I met the most wonderful nurse there. We immediately fell in love, and, well, to cut a long story short, last Saturday we got

married. Many of our friends say this was over-hasty, but I am convinced that our love will more than compensate for the difference between our social backgrounds and ethnic origins.

By this time, Mum and Dad, I suspect you may be getting a bit worried, so let me tell you straight away that everything I have written in this letter up to now is false. I made it up.

The truth is, two weeks ago I failed my final exams. I just want you to get this in the proper perspective.

Certainly there is evil and suffering in the world. We Christians cannot deny it. And if you want to allow it to make you cynical, you can. But Malachi wants you to get it in the right perspective. 'Surely the day is coming' (4:1). There is a reward for those who seek the face of God. Do not doubt it!

So we come to Malachi's final words. They constitute a postscript, not only to his prophecy, but to the whole Old Testament.

Obey the inspired word of God. Do not neglect it. 'Remember the law of my servant Moses, the decrees and laws I gave him at Horeb for all Israel' (4:4).

Be ready for the coming day of God. 'See, I will send you the prophet Elijah before that great and dreadful day of the LORD comes' (4:5).

Love one another earnestly, like members of a huge family. 'He will turn the hearts of the fathers to the children and the hearts of the children to their fathers' (4:6).

And *never, never surrender to that doubt which says the God of justice will not judge the world*. 'I will come and strike the land with a curse.'

Plenary evening meetings

I

The living word

by David Jackman

2 Timothy 3:1 – 4:8

In the fifteen months during which we've been planning Word Alive, I've been repeatedly reminded how desperately urgent is the need of our nation to hear the living word of God. And when we came to choose a title to sum up this week, I think we all felt that 'Word Alive' encapsulated our hopes and prayers for the week. I can't imagine a title more calculated to focus the great need of the church in our land and of our nation itself, that we should come under the living word of God. Everywhere we look in our culture we've seen signs of confusion and disintegration, yet in all the perplexity we find that many people resist the gospel with even greater determination. As questions are asked about our national situation, it often seems that people are saying, 'Any solution but the Christian one!'

In the months before this conference a couple of books have tried to do a hatchet job on the person of the Lord Jesus Christ and stage an assault on Christian standards and morality. Only this week, a new book by a psychiatrist has been announced, entitled *The End of Marriage: Why Monogamy Isn't Working*. The author proposes to expound his view of marriage as 'a damaging and outmoded institution which does more harm than good' – this when we live in a country where the crime rate soars, terrorism thrives and the Aids time bomb ticks on.

Not only does our culture appear to have no answers, but many people have given up hope that there ever could be such a thing as an answer. And in the midst of all this the Christian church's public image is that it is tongue-tied and embarrassed, shifting from one foot to another, dying the slow death of a thousand qualifications. So we have a senior church leader writing to a national newspaper saying that the murder of innocent children is really due to government economic policies, only to be rebuked by an atheist peer who says, 'Why is it that he doesn't believe any longer in sin?'

That is the situation in which we have to ask ourselves, 'What is the word from the Lord for us today?' That is what this week is all about, and I pray it will come to us, with a growing, burning conviction, that indeed there *is* a word from God. I hope that tonight, as we look at 2 Timothy, it will begin to become clear to us what that word may be. For these verses that we are considering are the apostle Paul's strategy for the last days.

Many of you will know that this is Paul's final letter; it's a stirring charge to a young pastor facing enormous challenges. Paul knows that his martyrdom is imminent. He says to Timothy, 'I am already being poured out like a drink offering, and the time has come for my departure' (4:6). This second letter of Timothy then is particularly concerned to keep this young pastor on track, and he wants the church at Ephesus, which he is serving, similarly to get its priorities clear. Though it's a personal letter written to one young man, the very last verse shows us that it's also written with the church in view: 'The Lord be with your spirit [singular]. Grace be with you [plural]' (4:22). So Paul wants the whole church to hear this letter and listen to his words to Timothy. Its primary application may well be to Christian leaders, but the wider scope is to all the members of the body of Christ.

This is the situation Paul is facing. What is his strategy for coping with the last days? He knows that it will not be long until his martyrdom. How is the young church going to be kept on course? How is it going to be faithful, not only in believing, but also in living this gospel of the grace of God? I believe that is a question tremendously relevant to us in our contemporary situation. So I want to draw out for you from this passage four great convictions, which I trust will be ours not only tonight but through this week and on into the rest of our lives, as we seek to be channels of the word of God and to learn that word better for ourselves so that we may live it and pass it on to others.

Convictions about the battle

I want to begin by taking you back to the beginning of chapter 3, where Paul says to Timothy, 'Mark this: there will be terrible times in the last days.' And this introduces an extremely important lesson: that in the last days, the focus of the battle will be inside the church as much as outside it. When you think about it, of course it's obvious that the enemy would use this as a primary tactic. If the church of Jesus Christ could be neutralized and rendered ineffective as God's change-agent for humanity, then the devil would have succeeded.

This is the warning Paul wants to sound. He uses the phrase 'the last days' in the sense in which the New Testament consistently uses it – to describe the period stretching from the ascension of the Lord Jesus Christ back to the glory that he had with the Father, to the very moment when he comes again in glory in his second advent. All of that, the New Testament says, is the 'last days', because God has done everything necessary to complete his purposes apart from sending his Son as king and judge.

Of course within the last days there are the 'last, last days', and it's very clear that what the Bible describes as last-day characteristics will then be particularly intensified. But what Paul is describing is not something that remote and far from Timothy. He's not looking forward 2,000 or more years. He is saying, 'These are battles that the church is always going to have to fight in every generation.' And the extraordinary thing is that in verse 5 he tells us that this battle is actually centred within the visible church of Jesus Christ. We find men and women 'having a form of godliness but denying its power'.

As a result, terrible times, or 'seasons of stress' as one translation puts it, will occur. We may well be in one of those times now. In 3:2–4 Paul gives us a devastating catalogue of the attitudes and behaviour that can be expected in such terrible times. I could easily illustrate that grisly list from our television screens and the newspapers of the last week or so. But I think it will be much more helpful to see what lies at the root of it all. *Why* does the church face this great battle?

Paul tells us very clearly, at the beginning of verse 2 and again at the end of verse 4: 'People will be lovers of themselves, lovers of money, . . . lovers of pleasure rather than lovers of God.' This is the heart of the problem, he says. Even within the church we shall be seduced into the wrong object of love. People who appear to be religious outwardly, who have a form of godliness, are nevertheless going to be diverted into loving themselves, money or pleasure instead of loving God. And that of course is the root of idolatry – putting created things in the place of the Creator. All those sins and vices of verses 2–4 flow from that corrupt centre. But the really startling thing (and this is what I want us to pick up, because it will be very important when we come to consider the remedy later), is that the location of the problem is apparently within the Christian community.

Now we can take it for granted that the world of irreligious people will manifest these characteristics, but it's the religion of the last days that particularly concerns Paul. For when God is dethroned at the very centre of our lives, religion doesn't disappear, it just becomes an empty shell. Outwardly it can often look exceedingly impressive – because that's all there is. There may be a great parade of Christian formalism; there can be all sorts of expressions of apparent Christian life within a community; there can be wonderful uplifting sermons and services; there can be all sorts of moral pronouncements made by the church. But, demands Paul, where is the demonstration of the power of the gospel? All the outward show lends a kind of credibility, but though the focus remains, the language is now almost empty.

We need to take that to heart, for we can see a good deal of this happening in the stress that we experience as God's people living in our particular generation. We're in the midst of all sorts of pressures, and the problems are not a million miles away from us, any more than they were from Timothy. It's not for us to point the finger at others; we can see the tensions in our own lives. As Christians we know how easily God is dethroned from the central position, how we start to revert to loving ourselves, to loving money, to loving pleasure; and how quickly our Christianity can become merely 'a form of godliness' lacking in real power. Paul wants us first of all to be convinced about the fact that there is a battle, and that the battle is not primarily 'out there' in the world, but 'in here' in our hearts. This battle, he wants us to know, is going on in the people of God; and he wants us to decide whether we are really going to let God be God at the very heart of our lives.

In verses 6–9, Paul goes on to talk about false teachers coming in and exploiting the weak, and false leaders resisting the truth. These problems all flow from the prevailing situation. Belief and behaviour are very closely linked. And it's because people's minds are corrupt that they resist the impact of God's truth and come to substitute their own false teaching and foolish ideas for God's revelation. So we must expect the church to be constantly engaged in that sort of battle; we must expect the pressure of the world around us to be constantly trying to squeeze us into its mould. (A church leader has said that the current religious climate in Britain might be summarized by the common assumption that it doesn't matter what you believe, so long as you believe it doesn't matter!)

We must expect this environment to be with us all the time. It's going to try to squeeze us into its mould. For however long we may have been Christians, however strongly we hold to the truth of the Bible, however enthusiastically we sing the great hymns and affirm the creeds and all the rest, we are not immune to these pressures. The seasons of stress are experienced within the church of Jesus Christ, and, says Paul, if we go down that route then we will be reprobate as far as the apostolic faith is concerned (verse 8). We will be men and women of depraved minds.

Convictions about the cost

Let's pick up Paul's argument at verse 10: 'You, however, know all about my teaching, my way of life, my purpose, faith, patience, love, endurance, persecutions . . . .'

Paul uses the little phrase 'but you' several times in the course of this short letter. The 'you' is emphatic, and here it introduces for Timothy a very strong contrast with all that has gone before. In the face of widespread decline in the church and rampant idolatry in the world, how is Paul going to cope? What is the future for the church of Jesus Christ?

'Well, Timothy,' he says, 'you've seen not only what I taught you, but also my way of life; you've seen that I have provided an exemplary outline around which you were able to trace the pattern of a godly life.' That's really what verse 10 means, when Paul says 'my way of life'. It is something that Timothy can trace, just as schoolchildren trace a map from an atlas through tracing paper. 'This is something I want you to remember,' says Paul. 'You know all about my teaching, you've heard me teach the gospel – but you've also seen my living.'

See how this theme runs through the passage. If the church is going to be authentic in the midst of battle, it isn't just a matter of knowing the teaching. It's a matter of living the teaching that we learn. Timothy has been privileged to know all about real Christian discipleship and authentic leadership, in Paul. And so Paul links those two things together: the doctrine is important and the lifestyle is important. 'And, Timothy, you've seen what wonderful qualities there are in my life – but have you noticed my persecutions and my sufferings? I want you to have some convictions, Timothy, about the cost.'

I believe that we Christians desperately need to renew our conviction about how costly it will be, and already is, to stand as a Christian in our society. The only answer to hypocrisy is reality, and the only remedy for false religion is the Lord Jesus Christ: but there is a cost involved. If you want to live a godly life, then you're not going to live it in the world unscathed. Verse 12: 'Everyone who wants to live a godly life in Christ Jesus will be persecuted.' That is why in verse 11 he reminds Timothy of what happened at Antioch where unbelieving Jews drove them out of the city, and at Iconium where there was a plot to stone Paul. At Lystra – where Timothy lived as a young man and so would have remembered the visit vividly – first they were received as gods, but then the religious men of the city initiated a riot and they stoned Paul and dragged him out of the city as if dead. And Paul says, 'Just remember, Timothy, what the cost of being a real Christian is, because you need to be a realist.' He will have none of the view that it's all going to be wonderfully easy and that we will float through all the difficulties. He wants to nerve us with some biblical realism. He tells us that we need to have convictions about the battle that's going on, and that we need to recognize the cost.

But do you notice something else in verse 11? It isn't Timothy's endurance that's important, so much as God's commitment to him. 'Yet the Lord rescued me from all of them.' That's the perspective in which he wants this young man to live. That's the right perspective to live by. We need this healthy biblical realism about living the Christian life. That's why we have this week in which to encourage one another and strengthen one another in our understanding of God's truth.

A godly life is always going to be a judgment on a self-centred life. But when self-centredness is accompanied by resistance to the truth, don't be surprised (verse 13) when evil, ungodly men and impostors go from bad to worse, deceiving and being deceived. 'But as for you,' says Paul, 'continue in what you have learned and have become convinced of, because you know those from whom you learned it' (3:14). Continue in it, even though evil impostors claim to go further, to go beyond the simple truth of the apostolic gospel; even though they tell you that they're getting nearer and nearer to God, while you, Timothy, are stuck with the apostle Paul in that old traditional type of Christianity.

Convictions about our great resource

Now we come to the heart of the passage. Paul's concern in verse 14 is obviously that Timothy is going to be swept away by some sort of novelty, that he will come under the influence of false teachers who will undermine his roots and cause him to drift him away from the gospel that Paul proclaimed; especially that gospel which he has been taught, through the Old Testament Scriptures, from the very godly influences of his childhood.

We know from 1:5 that both Timothy's grandmother and mother were sincere believers, and that they taught Timothy the Old Testament throughout his childhood. But the danger is that it can all sound very conservative and predictable and boring to some people.

I remember some years ago going on a training course for ministers who wanted to give local radio talks. We all had to write and deliver a short 'thought for the day'. There was a newly commissioned Salvation Army woman there who simply shared how she had been very deeply into the drug culture and how Christ had rescued her; but she didn't quite say it like that. She told us a little about her past, she told us where she was now, and then delivered her punchline: 'And all this change happened in my life through the Lord Jesus.' The producer-trainer for the day went bananas. He said, 'Oh, that's terrible, that's dreadful! It's so predictable and boring.'

Some of us rounded on him and said, 'You can't say that about a change in somebody's life like that!' But there is a great deal of that kind of thinking around; that it's predictable, that we've heard it all before.

I'm very impressed by how Paul remains strong on the things that Timothy has always learned and of which he has always been convinced. Timothy is not to abandon his convictions, both because of the quality of his teachers (his family and Paul), but supremely because of what he was taught. This is Paul's strategy. If the church in the last days is going to be faithful and true, it must recognize the battle that it's in; it has to count the cost of that battle; and it has to reaffirm its commitment to the one resource that God has given us, in order to guide and direct us in that battle. And that is what he calls, in verse 16, 'all Scripture'.

Timothy was taught the Old Testament, the holy Scriptures. Why is that important? Because, says Paul, they are 'able to make you wise for salvation through faith in Christ Jesus'. He is the heart of the biblical revelation. All the Old Testament points to him and finds its fulfilment in him. And this wisdom is not an intellectual, esoteric wisdom, it's a very practical, down-to-earth wisdom. This, says Paul, is how you come to salvation.

That's what all the false teachers lost sight of. They denied the power of the gospel. Their message wasn't able to bring salvation. So Timothy must go back to the message contained in the Old Testament in all the promises made from Abraham onwards about the way God was going to gather a covenant people and bless them, and the promise that through that covenant people all the nations of the world will be blessed. He must go back to those great promises that spoke of the gospel and that were fulfilled in Christ. It is all one plan, one great purpose of God from eternity to eternity. And if we do not have at the foundation of our belief this confidence in God's revelation in Scripture, then we shall be blown around everywhere by whatever sort of wind is blowing and by whoever seems to be the most powerful personality.

Of course Timothy knew that all the Scriptures were inspired by God. He'd probably had that conviction from childhood. So although verse 16 is a great statement about inspiration, notice that in its context it's actually a great statement about the profitability of Scripture. Paul is saying, 'This is your great resource. Faced with an unbelieving world and a church that is prone to heresy, there is a sufficient authority to keep the pastor and the people on track. What is it? It is all Scripture, it is the living word of God.'

That's the conviction that we're going to need, the conviction that we need to ask God to burn indelibly into our minds and hearts this week. All Scripture, says Paul, finds its origin in God. It is 'God-breathed'. So, just as my thoughts are carried on my breath to you in the form of words so that you can hear and relate to them, God carries his thoughts in words on the breath of his Spirit. He breathes out his mind in words. We don't have to grope after God and wonder if he's revealed himself to us or what he wants to say to us. He's said it clearly in the sixty-six books of the Bible, from Genesis to Revelation.

'All Scripture is God-breathed.' Paul is particularly thinking of the Old Testament. Jesus promised the apostles in the New Testament that the Holy Spirit would lead them into all truth (*cf.* Jn. 16:13). So we can have confidence in the word of God. And it is the mind of God that is being revealed. If I were breathing no breath, I can assure you that you would be hearing no words. If there were no Spirit working, then there would be no Bible. But the two together, the word and the Spirit, are the means by which God has revealed his mind infallibly and authoritatively to us. He has given us this great treasure, this amazing revelation, in order that we might know that every part of his revealed word is useful for 'teaching, rebuking, correcting and training'.

That's why we need to break down these foolish barriers that seem to have arisen between the word and the Spirit, as though there were some Christians who were 'word Christians' and others who were 'Spirit Christians' – and some who were 'truth Christians' and others who were 'love Christians'. I've heard people say it: 'Oh well, you're interested in doctrine, but I'm interested in experience', or 'They've got a Christian mind – but over here, we have a Christian heart.'

You can't separate the two like that! You can't separate the word from the Spirit, doctrine from experience, mind from heart. Word Alive exists not only to affirm the inspiration of the Bible, but to remind us of the sufficiency of the Bible for all our believing and behaving. That's the confidence that we evangelical Christians desperately need to recapture – that Scripture is the way by which God speaks infallibly to us, that it is in all Scripture that we can come to the touchstone of reality, and, of course, that what God breathes out is going to be profitable. Of course it is! Every part of it.

And because we know that 'what Scripture says, God says', and that (to paraphrase Jim Packer) the whole of the Bible is God preaching himself to us, then we need to have confidence in this great and sufficient answer, this limitless resource. That's why, in verse 16, Paul says, 'This is where we come to find God's authoritative word in terms of doctrine. Do you want to be taught? Well, all Scripture is there to teach you. Do you want to be trained in righteousness?' (You see, he's taking it from the doctrinal to the practical.) 'Well, it's in Scripture that you'll find that training.'

Those are the positives. But what if you need to be rebuked because you have wrong ideas? How is that going to happen? Only as you submit your mind to the authority of Scripture. Does your life need correcting? Of course it does, as mine does; we all need to be corrected day by day – from the Scriptures. Well then, that is the sufficient resource. Verse 17: 'so that the man [or woman] of God may be thoroughly equipped for every good work'. The sufficiency of the Bible – he is stressing it again.

Do you want to be thoroughly equipped to serve the Lord? Do you want everything that you will need to do every good work that God may call upon you to do? Where will you find that sufficiency? You'll find it in all Scripture. That is where God speaks his word. That is why the Holy Spirit has inspired the Scriptures, and as you ask God the Holy Spirit to illuminate your mind so that you can understand the Scripture, then you begin to have conviction about this great resource, this saving word of God that is inspired, sufficient and effective to equip us with everything good for doing God's will.

Before everything else, the man or woman of God is a man or woman of the Bible. That is the means by which the church is to be equipped for every good work. The Holy Spirit, the great author of Scripture, has given us this treasure through the human authors so that we might experience all God's resources which are being made available to us, to live a godly life in this world.

Convictions about our own priorities

Our time has almost gone, but I would like to etch on your minds the very solemn words of 4:1–2, as a focus for what we're going to be doing together in these next few days. What is Paul saying? He's saying, 'Put the Bible to work.' He's told us in 3:16 that it's effective for correcting and rebuking, for training and teaching. 'Well then, Timothy,' he says. 'This is your great priority as the pastor of this church in Ephesus. You must constantly be preaching that word. That's what you're called to do. That's what the ministry's all about – being a herald of God's truth.'

The tense of the verb implies that Paul sees Timothy at a crossroads, and that Timothy is being called upon to make a definite decision to adopt a certain course of action. Paul is saying, 'The only way you're going to be able to meet the crisis of the last days is if you, the pastor, preach the word so that the congregation is taught and corrected and rebuked and encouraged; and if you and I as hearers of that word receive it and respond to it in obedient faith and ask that same Holy Spirit to enable us to put it into practice in our lives.'

Now that requires great patience, does it not? It's not easy to sit and listen to the Bible being taught; it requires patience, humility and an active mind that sieves through what we hear and tests it against what Scripture is saying. I hope that will be characteristic of this week; that in all our seminar groups and plenary sessions you won't believe what the speaker says just because the speaker says it, but that you'll test it by the Scriptures, you'll go back to the word of God, you'll exercise your mind in God's word.

It requires patience, but also careful instruction. It sometimes requires patience on the preacher's part to continue preaching, but even more patience on the part of the congregation to continue listening. And it requires that together we should be careful about what we say and what we learn; for this is the word of the living God that we're handling, so it is a serious thing.

It is the great call to the pastor-teacher to be one who

preaches the word of God. Paul says (4:2): 'Stick at it, Timothy, whether you think it's an appropriate time or not; be prepared in season and out of season.' I want to encourage you this week to make time, in your own personal quiet times and in the sessions that you attend, however many or however few they may be, to listen to what God is saying through his word; to bring your mind under the authority of Scripture so that God's revelation may begin to direct us and to encourage and strengthen us. It will correct, it will rebuke, but it will also instruct. It will encourage. It will give us fresh vision. It will undergird us.

It is in the word of God that the power of God is seen. 'Oh,' people say, 'but they don't want that these days! Preaching's had it. People aren't interested in the Bible any more.'

But I think Paul would respond, 'Well, if you really think that, that makes it an even greater priority, doesn't it?' Verse 3: 'For the time will come when men will not put up with sound doctrine.' That's always been true in the church, at some times more than others. 'Instead, to suit their own desires, they will gather around them a great number of teachers to say what their itching ears want to hear.' Well, there's never been a shortage of that! Verse 4: 'They will turn their ears away from the truth and turn aside to myths.'

That's why you need to preach the word, Timothy. That's why you need to pray for your pastor back at home and to encourage him to be a preacher of the word of God. That's why we need to be hearing that word, learning it together, demanding that we might understand it better. For there will always be false prophets in the church, just as there were in Old Testament times, people who will tell others exactly what they want to hear. They'll adapt the Christian message to the prevailing culture; they'll accommodate the good news to the agenda of those who are lovers of self, money and pleasure. You can see that sort of prostitution of the gospel all around us today.

'But you,' says Paul to Timothy in verse 5, 'keep your head in all situations, endure hardship, do the work of an evangelist, discharge all the duties of your ministry.' We're all called to different tasks and to different ministries; we all have different gifts. But we all have a part to play in the church of the Lord Jesus Christ and we're all called to be people who think biblically, whose minds are given to the truth, who hold on soberly to God's revelation in every area. We're not to be surprised when it's hard, when we suffer, when we get flack for it. That was Timothy's experience, and it's always been the experience of faithful men and women. But we're to keep the gospel at the heart of what we do in our churches. We're to do the work of evangelists; we're to keep on gospelling day by day, and we are to seek to fulfil the task the Lord has given us.

He has given each of us gifts to use within his church. And whatever those gifts may be, they are all to the end that the word of the Lord may sound out from churches that not only believe the truth but live it, and from lives that are living demonstrations of the power of the word of God in practice. Friends, if we are to meet the enormous challenges of this hour we must make those priorities ours; we must return to these scriptural priorities, to these paths of the Bible.

And if we do that, and if this week we renew with one another – in our personal fellowship, as we listen to God's word, as we pray and think things through – this sense of conviction about the battle, the cost, the resources, the great power of the word of God to transform people's lives, the great commitment of the Holy Spirit to use that word to bring the dead to life and make even people such as us more and more like the Lord Jesus; and if we have conviction that that should be our priority – then in our own lives and, please God, in our churches, we shall see a demonstration in new ways of the word of the Lord speeding on and triumphing. As Paul said to the Thessalonians, the word of God will have free course and be glorified (*cf.* 2 Thes. 3:1).

For it still is the power by which God reveals himself, and by which he changes human lives. That's his strategy for the last days, and I believe it's his strategy for our days together this week.

2

The great God

by Nigel Lee

Isaiah 40

What a great chapter of encouragement! Here is God working to encourage a particular people in a very particular situation. We're in the eighth century BC. Isaiah had been called to be a prophet in 742, the year that King Uzziah died. He was a great servant of God, faithful in a period of growing spiritual decline.

The first thirty-nine chapters of the book of Isaiah spell out God's charges against not only his own people, but against some of the surrounding nations. The climax comes in 39:5, when Isaiah says to Hezekiah:

> Hear the word of the LORD Almighty: The time will surely come when everything in your palace, and all that your fathers have stored up until this day, will be carried off to Babylon. Nothing will be left, says the LORD. And some of your descendants, your own flesh and blood who will be born to you, will be taken away, and they will become eunuchs in the palace of the king of Babylon.

'You will be driven into exile, your relatives will be taken away and mutilated and Jerusalem will be sacked.' What had happened to bring God's people to such a state?

He called Abraham originally out of Mesopotamia, up in the north. He brought the people through their experiences in Egypt into this land. He established the city of Jerusalem, 'my city, I will put my name there' – God actually picked it out, and placed his people all around. He had protected that city. Here was his home on earth; he had said, 'I will live among you, you will be my people, I will be your God.' Here at the heart of Jerusalem was established the place of

99

sacrifice where people could come to meet with God; guilty of sin, stained and muddy in their consciences, they could come bringing their sacrifices and offer them up. Here was the very gateway of heaven to them, the place of restored fellowship with God. They could hear the priest say, 'Your sins are forgiven.'

If they lost that, where would they turn? In this city, this holy place, the very symbols of the covenant that God had made with them were present in the ark. What memories they had of that long wilderness journey, when even their shoes didn't wear out, right through into this land, into Jerusalem, the very home of God! This was where the word of God was to be taught and heard and was to ripple out around the nation, and through them to the other nations around. In this city, Solomon had built his temple on the mount; in 1 Kings 8:10, the glory of the Lord had come down and filled that place. The priests had to get out. God was there, on earth, the Creator. And as the years went by and the centuries succeeded each other, their faith in that God became shallower. They stopped listening so closely to his word. They didn't really know him. It was like a marriage (as we were thinking of in Malachi this morning) that remains technically faithful, but has actually become frigid and frozen.

Somebody has estimated that the average length of time that British married couples speak to each other is approximately 55 minutes a week, and in America only 27 minutes. Such a distance had been growing between God and his people; their leaders were becoming corrupt; the people needed protection from them more than from the surrounding nations. The house of God was gradually falling into disrepair and the religious feasts which God had established were forgotten. The word of God was disregarded; in its place, the worship of Baal was actually creeping right in to the temple. Of course the language was the same; they would still talk about 'the Lord', but the meaning had changed. And cultic homosexuality was being endorsed from the top down and practised all around the temple. Child sacrifice was spreading again on the nation's borders.

Mediums and spiritualists were beginning to fasten on to people's fears. Because the word of God was not heard in the land, by the time of Josiah they had lost it altogether. They had only one copy left, and it had to be rediscovered.

Any church, denomination, parachurch organization or mission where even a part of this process takes place must face what happened to Israel. The Lord said he would remove his protection. If they were not prepared to honour him and listen to his word, he would remove his blessing from them and allow the temple to be ruined. He would allow the sacrifices to be stopped and the people to be taken all the way back to Mesopotamia whence they came. If they were not prepared to live as God's own holy people, then he would let them be treated as if they were no different from any other. The words of Isaiah in chapter 39 must have come as a terrible shock: to be taken back to Babylon, to have nobody left of your family, to see your own kith and kin become mere eunuchs in a pagan tyrant's palace.

And now Isaiah's book and ministry turn a corner. Like a true prophet, he brings the people not only the warnings against the drifting, the malaise that is eating like a cancer into their spiritual lives and behaviour; but he prepares them for what is to come. Amos says, 'The Sovereign LORD does nothing without revealing his plan to his servants the prophets' (Am. 3:7). Isaiah is beginning now to prepare the people for their return; to bring to them in exile a message of hope, restoration and repentance so that they needn't simply despair and be defeated.

Isaiah is looking down the years and preparing them for what's coming, for a new start when the exile is all over. He is dealing with the guilt, the shock of realizing that God could treat them like this, that disasters like this could be allowed; dealing with the hurts and the fears that these cataclysmic events will have caused. Sometimes such awful things happen to us that we feel numbed inside, hardly able to respond or even to listen. Moses came to the people when they were slaves: 'God has a message for you: he says, "I'm going to get you out of all this, you're going to be free, I'm going to take you to your own land, I will live with you and dwell with you."' He reported this to the Israelites, 'but they did not listen to him because of their discouragement and cruel bondage' (Ex. 6:9).

I don't know what is going on in your own home or church. Perhaps you've come here chilled and numbed by things that have happened in your own witness; things you've done and will perhaps remember with regret for the rest of your life. Perhaps you are bruised by damage in your home, splits in your own church. And you cannot even start to listen to what you know God wants to say, because of the numbing effect of the trauma and the pain that you've just been through.

'Comfort,' says the Lord, and repeats it. 'Have you got it? I want to comfort you, I want to encourage you. Oh Jerusalem, I want to speak tenderly to you; will you listen to me?' This is awesome. That God should speak like this, of himself, to these people after all that they have done to him!

I want to look with you at seven things that God says of himself to people like this, in crisis.

God has dealt with your sin (verse 2)

Sin is what had caused all the trouble, and now it had finally come to a head: this rebellion, this hardened heart. 'You went your own way, you didn't listen. You sinned quite deliberately. God has dealt with it, in two ways. First, you have had hard service in your captivity – but it's got through to you and your hearts have been softened. It's all over; you've done your time, and now you're out. It's finished. God has accomplished his chastening. But he has also forgiven you. Sin is paid for.'

This is the starting point of any way back to God: hearing those five words, 'Sin has been paid for.' A few years ago, I had a real problem with the Inland Revenue. I wasn't paying tax and hadn't done so for years. I didn't earn enough to do so. They said it would cost more just to attend to my papers than they could ever hope to get back off me in tax, and they asked me not to send tax returns to them.

Then my circumstances changed, and I had to start dealing with the tax man. It was a frightening experience! I had no tax number, my affairs were in complete confusion, I couldn't even understand the forms (for me, mathematics is one of the results of the fall). So I was really panicking when a friend visited me. He was a businessman who had come to Christ through the work in our church a year or two previously. He listened my tale of woe, then said, 'I want you to do just one thing. Let me take your papers to my accountant. He'll deal with it and it won't cost you anything.'

I went with him to his godless, rugby-playing accountant, explained my situation with some difficulty – living by faith wasn't a concept he found very easy to grasp – and finally he said, 'This won't be a problem. I'll deal with it.' I walked home on air. It was incredible: I didn't have to pay a thing, it was all dealt with.

I wonder – do you know, off by heart, the terms of the new covenant? You can find them in Hebrews, quoted from Jeremiah 31: 'I will put my laws in their minds and write them on their hearts. I will be their God, and they will be my people . . . They will all know me, from the least of them to the greatest. For I will forgive their wickedness and will remember their sins no more' (Heb. 8:10–12). That is a covenant, a legal document drawn up by the greatest lawyer in the universe, and I am so glad that he puts that bit about forgiveness at the bottom, not at the top. For it would have been so easy for us to think, 'God says he will forgive – wonderful! But then he writes his laws in our minds and hearts, and we fail . . . .' But he puts the forgiveness at the bottom, after he has written of his own purposes and plans and laws in our minds and hearts. He is a God of forgiveness. He deals with these things utterly.

He is coming back (verses 3–5)

Secondly, the Lord says, 'I'm coming back to Jerusalem.' There is a voice crying, 'Prepare the way for the LORD, through the desert.' Verse 5: 'The glory of the LORD will be revealed, and all mankind together will see it.'

Perhaps they thought he would never come to see them

again. Not in the old way. And why should he? They've
brought idols right into the temple and turned their back on
him. They didn't want to know him any more. And after all
that, the Lord says: 'I'm coming back to you – prepare the
way, clear out the stones, flatten down the bumps,
straighten out the road.'

He's going to reveal his glory again, but on an even vaster
scale now for us than he did for them in Jerusalem. The Lord
came, and revealed his glory. John 1:14: 'The Word became
flesh and made his dwelling among us.'

'And we,' says John, 'I and the other apostles, we have
seen his glory, the glory of the One and Only, who came
from the Father, full of grace and truth.' Many didn't see it.
'He came to that which was his own, but his own did not
receive him. Yet to all who received him, to those who
believed in his name, he gave the right to become the
children of God' (Jn. 1:11–12). Those few could go around
then, moving out from Jerusalem: 'We've seen his glory full
of grace, he's full of truth, listen to what he says!' And they
went crying in the wilderness, to the uttermost parts of the
earth – and one day now, says Isaiah, the Lord will come
again on a vast scale and every eye will see his glory.

Won't that be tremendous? Every single person will see it!
And he adds: just in case you have a scrap of doubt left in
your heart, 'the mouth of the LORD has spoken'. There is
nothing surer. It will happen; the Lord is coming back.
These pictures given to God's people and the encouragement brought to them are models for us: the thing will
happen on a world-wide scale.

His word lives for ever (verses 6–8)

One of the questions for those returning from exile might
well have been: 'Whom do we trust now? We trusted our
leaders, the kings appointed over us; they betrayed us.
Their glory was a lightweight thing, here today and gone
tomorrow, just like the flowers of the field. So whom do we
trust now?' And the prophet says, 'Wherever you go to,
don't trust in princes, don't even trust in your leaders, if you
trust in them more than the word of God. Trust in the word

of God that is in them, the word they bring to you, the word that will stand for ever.'

The apostle Peter takes this up when in 1 Peter 1:22–25 he quotes, most illuminatingly, these same verses from Isaiah. 'You have been born again,' he says. How? Every single one here was born again because the word of God, the living, eternal word of God, at some point took root in you. It is that which lives and endures. Your glory will tarnish and grow mildewed and blow away. It is the word of God in us that generates eternal, spiritual life in you and in your brothers and sisters around you.

You've started to love them, says Peter. 'Love one another' (verse 22). They're eternal like you, they are part of God's eternal riches; so don't damage them.

As a child I had the privilege of working on my uncle's farm in the Lake District over a number of holidays at lambing time. Sometimes, I remember, the ewe would die giving birth and you would be left with a tiny, soggy orphaned lamb. Often the same night another ewe would survive and its lamb die. In such cases we would take the dead lamb and skin it, and fit its skin over the live lamb – it was a pretty tight fit, but we'd do it – and bring the living lamb to the living mother to try to get it to suckle. When, a few days later, the mother could smell its own milk in the orphaned lamb, the bonding was complete. We could clip off the borrowed skin then: an unbreakable bond had been established. The ewe would never turn it away; it smelt its own life in the lamb.

God plants his eternal word in us, he knows it's there. Cities collapse, whole peoples are driven off into exile and then brought back, we live through turmoil and confusion and persecution – and Isaiah says, 'The word of the Lord in you – listen to it, digest it, feed upon it, make it part of yourself. That is what lives for ever! Get it inside you.'

He is a king with the heart of a shepherd (verses 9–11)

At the end of verse 9, Isaiah says: 'Here is your God!' He's the sovereign Lord, all his power lies at his disposal, his sleeves are rolled up, his arm rules for him, his reward is with him (it would be tremendous to talk about the whole doctrine of rewards, but we have no time). And God – so powerful, and the one who is coming – behaves like a shepherd (verse 11). This great sovereign God knows our needs as intimately as a shepherd those of his flock.

'He gently leads those that have young.' Often, particularly with a first child, a mother can feel that her spiritual life has come up against a brick wall. Bible reading goes out of the window, for it's so difficult when you have no energy and your nights are disturbed. Some church activities that were very important to you are suddenly no longer possible. Many a young mum, when the first baby comes along, reaches a point of hurt and confusion for she feels that somehow she has stopped walking with God in the way she knew. And God understands this. He says that he gently leads those that have young. Perhaps there is just one person here for whom that truth is a special comfort. He knows about your situation. The Lord will walk you at the pace you are able to walk. He gently leads the flock along, especially those that have young stumbling along with them. This is your God.

I wish you could have seen the drama we had last night in the students' celebration. It portrayed two angels manning the gates of heaven. It was just after the crucifixion. They were deeply disturbed at the sight of the first person to arrive: the dishevelled, untaught thief, who had just been put to death for trying to rob Pontius Pilate's palace. His understanding of theology was not great; he was immediately attracted to the possibility of knocking off a few things in heaven. The angels tried to keep this unusual man out. Eventually one of them had to go and ask for higher instructions. He came back very embarrassed.

Behold your God! He shepherds you, a hurting, needy, stumbling, weak-kneed one, though he is the sovereign God.

He is a great God (verses 12–17)

God is so great, say these next verses, that you can hardly imagine it. All the oceans of the world he simply holds in the palm of his hand. He's as great as that. He measures the expanse of the heavens with the breadth of his hands.

When my oldest daughter was learning to count, she was very proud of her ability to count up to seven. One night I took her out of doors for a night-time walk.

'Can you count, Ali?' I asked.

'Yes!'

'Can you count the stars?'

'Yes!'

'Start,' I said.

She looked up at the night sky and began: '1–2–3–4–5–6 . . . *Aaaah!*' She had suddenly seen the splash of the Milky Way across the sky.

God measured the expanse of the heavens with the breadth of his hands; he can pack all the dust of the earth into his shopping basket. Can you imagine that? All the mountains of the world he puts on his kitchen scales. What a great God! You know, if you reduced our galaxy, if you shrank it down to the size of Europe, our sun would be like a speck of dust and this planet would be invisible. And there are numerous galaxies we don't even know, each a minimum of two million light years away from the next.

God is so great. And he looks after young mums with their kids who cry in the night. He is that kind of a God. 'I am the high and lofty one,' he says, 'and I attend to the needs of the widows and the orphans.' Nobody has taught God anything. Whole nations are just like a heap of house dust (verse 15)!

He is incomparable (verses 18–26)

Verse 25: he 'brings out the starry host one by one, and calls them each by name'; he treats them like sheep. He knows them all; and the amazing thing is that this God – this king, this Saviour shepherd, this creator of such vastness – will one day share the government of this universe with you and me.

Imagine going round one of those enormous, palatial stately homes and looking at all the various art treasures, the carpets and so on; and you happen to meet the owner. You fall into conversation with him and you really get on very well with him; after a while he says he would like to show you some of the hidden treasures that are not generally open to the public. He gives you a most fascinating tour of all kinds of other treasures. And then he says, 'Now – would you like to become the part-owner of all of this, with me?'

That is what God has done. He has sent his Son in order to tear down that law which stood between us and him; to bring us a free, lasting, forgiveness of sins. And now we've come to know him, and he's put his word in us and his Spirit in us. 'Have a look at some of these heavens; have a look at these nations; draw up close to me, because I want to share the government of all this with you.' This is our God. A God who would send his Son, the Son who volunteered to come; they are so at one, that he came and gave his life so that we might be rescued from sin and guilt and lostness. He puts his word in us, and he gathers us in his flock.

He is a God who cares (verses 27–31)

So, says verse 27, why are you complaining? 'Why do you say, O Jacob, and complain, O Israel, "My way is hidden from the LORD . . .?"' Why do you feel hard done by or think that God has somehow mislaid you, that he doesn't know where you've come to this week, which seat you're sitting on, which chalet you're going to try to find your way back to later on. Do you think God doesn't know these things? And the tensions at home, the problems in the church, the fears of unemployment, the difficulties in recession and the big questions that you're facing in your life? – do you think God doesn't care, that he doesn't know?

How could a God who could make all this, and yet be so attentive to detail, grow tired or weary? Are you doubting your own resources, facing some new challenge and thinking you haven't got what it takes? This passage is so realistic. 'Even youths grow tired and weary' – even the elite, the super-fit crack troops, and 'young men stumble and fall; but those who hope in the LORD' – those who trust in him and draw near to him, who chew on his word, who feed on it and talk of it with their friends – 'they will soar on wings like eagles; they will run and not grow weary.'

I spend a lot of my time trying to explain the gospel to roomfuls of godless students around the universities and colleges of this country. It's a fascinating, challenging job, and a ministry for which I am so grateful to God. I see the real hard nuts coming in. They sit down near the back, near the door. They chew their gum and drink their beer and they look at me and say, 'Go on, give us your best shot.'

I open up the Bible and I preach the Bible to them, and I watch. And as I am preaching I am watching what is going on in them. They start to concentrate. The jaws move more slowly, and the beer remains half-drunk. They go pale, their faces drop; I'm thinking, even as I'm preaching, 'Hit them again, Lord! Hit them, keep hitting them!'

One fellow turned his life over to Christ just a few months ago in Exeter. He came along to a number of meetings wearing a big England rugby shirt. (This was before England had lost to Wales!) He used to sit there, very macho. On the Friday night of that mission week he came to see me afterwards. He was just broken down by what he had been hearing over the previous few days, and he wanted to give his life utterly to Christ.

He was like three other fellows I remember just a fortnight later. They came up together like the front row of a rugby scrum; they'd almost got their arms around each other as they came to see me. They said, 'We've been talking about this and we've decided that it's true and we want to become Christians. What do we do?'

It is so thrilling to be able to preach the word of God and see God changing people. That first man in Exeter wrote to me a week or two later. He said, 'I am so grateful for what I learnt that week from Luke's gospel. I've given my life to Christ. I really think I ought to become a missionary – where should I go?' He'd only been a Christian two weeks. Those young fellows, so enthusiastic as they've listened to the Scriptures; they've heard God speaking, they've chewed it over, watched their friends, been given an opportunity quietly to make a response; and with dignity and honesty, they've done it.

I know they're going to get tired, I know they're going to come under attack, I know things are not going to be easy in the universities of this country. Pray for those who are in the student meeting, in another part of this conference taking place right now, for they are fighting on one of the battle-fronts that really count.

And yet, even when the 'young men', the leaders – young men and women – of the Christian Unions get weary, are tired and feel they've got nothing left, then, if only they will feed on the word of God, if only they will look up to the One who created the heavens, they'll know that he is a God of forgiveness, a God who comes.

'But those who hope in the LORD will renew their strength. They will soar on wings like eagles; they will run and not grow weary, they will walk and not be faint.'

Behold your God – and worship him!

3

The great need

by Dick Lucas

Psalm 51:17

Turn with me, please, to this great penitential psalm, and to verse 17, our key verse for tonight: 'The sacrifices of God are a broken spirit; a broken and contrite heart, O God, you will not despise.'

That seems to me to be a verse of extraordinary beauty and power, and evidently the NIV translators felt the same because it is virtually unchanged from the old Authorized Version. Perhaps they felt they would only spoil it by handling it, and I feel rather like that tonight!

But I trust that I am not going to spoil it for you, but clarify it and unfold it so that you will never forget it. If you forget my words tonight, that doesn't very much matter – as long as you don't forget these wonderful words of verse 17. Take them away with you tonight in your mind and in your memory; repeat them as you get up in the morning and as you go to bed at night, and speak them to one another: 'The sacrifices of God are a broken spirit; a broken and contrite heart, O God, you will not despise.'

Now what we have here is one description, out of many, of a worshipper. Verse 17 marks the point the penitent has reached in his journey as he anticipates forgiveness. You'll see that in verse 14 he is asking to be saved from bloodguilt so that his tongue will sing of God's righteousness; that is surely worship. He says in verse 15, 'O LORD, open my lips, and my mouth will declare your praise.' He talks about God not delighting in sacrifice, 'or I would bring it' – that is the language of worship – and then he says he wants to bring a sacrifice, the sacrifice of a broken spirit. So the psalmist at this point is talking about worship.

Worship has been the subject of great debate and teaching in the last twenty years, and rightly so. But the Bible student will take all that discussion back to the Bible as the measuring rod. How does God see it all? What is acceptable in his sight? What is his understanding of worship? In what terms does his word define the true worshipper? And here is just one outstanding example of how God defines the true worshipper.

It seems to me that there is a possibility of misunderstanding both this verse and the whole psalm, both in ancient Old Testament times and in modern Christian times.

Misunderstanding in an ancient context

First in the Old Testament. From your reading of Isaiah, some of the other eighth-century prophets and Psalm 50 (and again there is an echo of it in verse 16), you're probably familiar with passages where it seems that the prophets and psalmists are conspiring to do away with the sacrificial system which God had established. It seems as though, speaking in the name of God, they disapproved of the sacrifices that the people were bringing. And it was a very different situation from that of Malachi which we've been hearing about in the morning Bible readings. You remember that the worshippers were weary with their worship; they were bored and apathetic. But when we come to these great statements about sacrifice in the prophets and the psalms, we're being told not so much that the worshipper is weary, bored and apathetic, but that it is God who's weary. Neither is the worship second-rate, as it was in Malachi's day. According to our understanding of it, it was first-rate. In the best sense you could call it cathedral worship; you could say it was the finest of Spring Harvest singing with 3,000 full-throated people at Word Alive.

With music of that standard and everyone's hearts apparently in it, it is remarkable to hear the divine antagonism to it. I'm sure you're familiar with Isaiah's words in his first chapter:

'The multitude of your sacrifices –
    what are they to me?' says the LORD.

'I have more than enough of burnt offerings,
    of rams and the fat of fattened animals;
I have no pleasure
    in the blood of bulls and lambs and goats.
When you come to appear before me [that is, with your
        worship, your singing, your wonderful music],
    who has asked this of you,
    this trampling of my courts?
Stop bringing meaningless offerings!
    Your incense is detestable to me.
New Moons, Sabbaths and convocations [endless
        services] –
    I cannot bear your evil assemblies . . .
    my soul hates [them].
They have become a burden to me;
    I am weary of bearing them.'

                                                        (Is. 1:11–14)

Isn't that extraordinary language? It is, if you like, the other side of the coin: not now the people of God weary of worship, but God weary of listening to them.

Now, how can this be, that in these great prophetic writings and in the Psalms God appears to weary of the worship that he has ordained and commanded from his people? I think a moment's thought will make it very clear to any Bible student. It is not that God is repudiating the sacrificial system. What he is repudiating (and it is crucially important to realize it) is making worship a substitute for obedience, devotion and righteousness. It's worth taking a moment to recognize the link, unique in the ancient world, that the Bible makes between religion and ritual on the one hand, and righteousness and holiness on the other. It was a link unknown in other ancient religions, and is unknown in many ethnic religions today.

The writings of Stephen Neill have helped me particularly on this point. You come across the holy man begging in India, but if you don't give him money you'll find that his language is appalling. In Hinduism, as in many other languages, the link between being a 'holy man' and practical holiness as we understand it has never been made. It is something that is unique to the Bible.

What then God is rebuking is religion without righteousness. So what is it, according to verse 17, that God says is essential in anybody who claims to be a Christian worshipper? The answer is, many things; but it is essential to have a broken spirit and a contrite heart.

Misunderstanding in a modern context

In modern times also and in our own culture there is the possibility of grievous misinterpretation, as I want to make abundantly plain.

I looked up the word 'broken' in my *Thesaurus*, and found under heading 3 the following words for brokenness and contrition: 'enfeebled, weakened, crushed, defeated, dispirited, dejected, discouraged and demoralized'. Just take those five 'd's'. Is this what pleases almighty God – that the worshippers who come into his presence should be defeated, dispirited, dejected, discouraged and demoralized? Is that your idea of what God wants at the heart of your life? If so, one would have to call God sadistic, which God forbid.

You will be glad to know that I took another look at my *Thesaurus*, and found under heading 4 the following (and what a world of difference!): 'trained, disciplined, obedient, docile, subdued'. Now that may not be quite what I'm after, but it's obvious that what is in David's mind is something very like that second list: beautiful qualities of modesty and meekness, lowliness and humility. And I need hardly say, for you know it in yourself and in others, these are not natural to us as fallen creatures. This is the opposite of that which lies deep within us all, that which is disdainful of others, egotistical, conceited, self-satisfied, vainglorious, cocky and on the make for number one, even using Christ to give us a leg-up.

Now what is being talked about here in verse 17 is something akin to the beauty of the Lord Jesus Christ who was meek and lowly of heart (Mt. 11:28, AV). It is the unfading beauty of Christian womanhood that Peter has the nerve to name as a gentle and a quiet spirit (1 Pet. 3:4). It is the attractiveness of the Lord's servant, the man of God, the Christian leader in 2 Timothy, who is gentle to all, even to those who oppose the truth (2 Tim. 2:24). It is precisely that quality which Isaiah celebrates in one of the greatest of his great passages: 'This is what the high and lofty One says – he who lives for ever, whose name is holy: "I live in a high and holy place, but also with him who is contrite and lowly in spirit, to revive the spirit of the lowly"' (Is. 57:15).

That, then, is what we're talking about: this essential thing that is not natural to us, that can be wrought in us only by the work of God: essentially we're to come into God's presence and praise his name. How can such a spirit, so alien to me by nature, be worked in me?

I want to issue a warning.

As I talk about these beautiful qualities, I'm quite sure in some of you there will be a fresh desire welling up, even at this very moment, in holy resolutions to be like this. I want to say right at the beginning that it's not in your power to do this, and these resolutions may not be very helpful.

I remember when I was young you often had in Christian meetings and conventions a 'consecration evening'. The appeal was made to surrender absolutely everything afresh to God. Such meetings impress me less and less, in terms of their theological content. I realize sometimes there is something stubborn in our lives that does need to be handed over to God absolutely. But I've grown a little weary of the clichéd terminology of the consecration meeting. The claim that we can, that very evening and for ever, make Christ Lord is not one that I find to be true to myself or to my Christian neighbour.

When we take a closer look at reality, at our own Christian experience and at the experience of Christians whose testimony we value, we find that the whole movement is actually very different, indeed it is the other way round. It is not we who are making Christ Lord, it is he, the Lord, who is making us into his servants. That is the meaning of your life. That is what is happening to you. From the moment God laid his hands upon you, from the moment you were regenerated, he has been in the process of making you a satisfactory servant of his; and indeed, it will take a lifetime. And whether you respond willingly or unwillingly makes very little difference, except that if you're unwilling the chastening will be much sterner.

The process by which Christ the Lord makes us his servants is delineated in some measure in this great psalm. Obviously it's a very long psalm, and I'm going be selective. As I try to find in Psalm 51 the method that God uses to make me of a broken and a contrite spirit, humble and lowly and pleasing to him, I'm going to find two revelations, each with their appropriate two responses.

Let me explain those terms. The Psalms are – virtually uniquely – both revelation and response. They are a revelation of God's truth to us; we learn about God from the Psalms just as from any other book in holy Scripture.

It has always been amazing to me that the young monk Martin Luther learnt as much from the Psalms as he did from the epistle to the Romans. It was from the Psalms that he learnt so much about justification; it was from the Psalms that he learnt so much about God, that revolutionized all the thinking that he'd had until that time.

So the Psalms are a revelation of God; we shall learn about him tonight. But they're also always a response; they are the prayer and praise book of Israel and now of the universal church. And for every conceivable feeling, experience and situation in which we find ourselves we can find words appropriate and sufficient in these Psalms. People say, 'I don't know where to find words with which to speak of such a great God; there are no human words adequate.' That is not true. God has given us words in the Psalter, words by which we may come to him when we're full of joy or full of sorrow; when we're rebellious or when we're obedient; there are words for every kind of situation in the Christian life from beginning to end.

So tonight we're going to look at two revelations and two responses, and as we look at them you will see how God humbles us and makes us the kind of people he wants us to be. And the first revelation is this.

God's revelation of the extraordinary power of sin and evil

The extraordinary power of sin and evil is not really on the world's agenda at all, though it has recently raised itself with the death of little James Bulger.[1] It almost seems that many people have awoken from a deep sleep. People have been speaking to each other on street corners in a state of shock about this awkward subject that doesn't usually appear in grocery-shop conversation: evil in our society and in people's lives. How could children do this? What is this evil that is proliferating in our society?

Historians are even now clearing their desks and licking their pencils in preparation to write the history of the twentieth century. One of the great problems they're going to face is this awful spectre of evil. There has never been a century so full of wars and terrifying cruelty. The Holocaust, refugees, torture – you name it, our century puts all others in the shade. It is extremely humiliating for progressive, enlightened modern man.

But of course Psalm 51 is not talking about the power of evil in society that has raised its ugly head so much in recent weeks. It is talking about the power of sin and evil within the kingdom of God. David was a man after God's own heart; and now he was an adulterer, and yes, I have to say it, a murderer. And he doesn't stand alone in the pages of Scripture; the extraordinary truthfulness of the Bible writers enables us to see into the lives of Abraham, Noah, Moses, Peter and many more biblical heroes, and find things that we would never dream of putting into the lives of our heroes if we wanted people to praise them and look up to them.

Many years ago, when I was very young and perhaps

---

1. The reference is to a tragic event in February 1993 when a toddler, James Bulger, was abducted and murdered. Two boys, aged ten at the time, were later found guilty. The case was widely reported and provoked a national outcry, with calls for greater policing and claims of a breakdown of national morality.

rather too theologically well-read for my age, I had been reading through a lengthy tome on indwelling sin. And I had been listening, at a very big meeting, to a propounder of the higher-life teaching, which claimed that if you had sufficient faith in the power of the Holy Spirit you could come out of the wretched experiences of Romans 7 into the glorious liberty of the children of God in Romans 8.

I was very young, and I don't say this to my credit. Perhaps I was a little cocky. But later that evening after the meeting had finished I questioned the speaker. I said that it didn't seem to me to fit into what I'd been reading: did we really leave Romans 7 behind? And we walked and walked and talked and talked, and I was astonished (and, I may say, deeply impressed) when the speaker said to me, 'Dick, I say that sentence of Paul's from Romans 7 – "What a wretched man I am!" – almost every day of my life.'

I don't know what strange divisions in the mind permit one to say something on a platform that is not actually true in our experience. I think it was because it was a tradition that he was speaking to, and we almost persuade ourselves that our traditions must be true. But the moment we looked at it and talked together, out of the heart of this very godly man and very experienced Christian came the honest statement, that almost every day of his life he said to himself: 'What a wretched man I am! Who will rescue me from this body of death?' (Rom. 7:24).

Of course Romans 8 speaks of the power of the indwelling Holy Spirit; but it never denies the power of indwelling sin and the resulting conflict in the Christian's life. What a revelation David's sin was to him: 'I know my transgressions, and my sin is always before me . . .' (Ps. 51:3). It's almost as though this is a fresh knowledge, a revelation that he'd hardly suspected before, and now he acknowledges it: 'I know it, I cannot avoid it any longer; it is staring me in the face; I have to say I know my heart in a way that I had not known it before.'

Verse 4: 'Against you, you only, have I sinned and done what is evil in your sight, so that you are proved right when you speak and justified when you judge.' That is the very opposite of us. Everybody tells us that they don't deserve to be punished by God, that it's ridiculous to suppose that a loving God would punish them. The man in the street would be enormously annoyed at the very idea that he was a hell-deserving sinner: 'It's just a hackneyed formula.'

What an extraordinary thing, then, to come to a position of maturity in your life where you can honestly look at your own sins, then look into the face of God and say, 'If you judged me worthy of hell, you would be right.' Verse 5: I know surely that all my life long I haven't had to learn evil, it has been endemic in my heart. Verse 6: all that dissembling, all that deceit and covering-up – I'm now aware of it and I know now that you want to teach me wisdom in that heart of the whole matter, within.

In other words, to put it very simply, David has come to a new self-knowledge. There is a sense in which Christianity and Christian experience can do what a thousand psychologists can't do. They can introduce you to yourself. Thus God deals with all of us in different ways and over different periods, with the one aim that we shall come to a true self-knowledge. Our hearts are deceitful above all things and desperately wicked, and until you know that, you haven't begun to grow up as a Christian. That was the revelation that God made to David when he sent Nathan the prophet to him, and began by his Spirit to work in him an acknowledgment of what he had never really acknowledged before – his dreadful wickedness within his heart (2 Sa. 12:1–13).

David's response of extraordinary pain and agonizing grief

Now what was David's response to all this? Look at verse 8. He longs to hear again joy and gladness; 'Let the bones you have crushed rejoice.' He feels absolutely crushed, he has an almost unappeased pain, and with the pain there is an awful fear. Is he going to be cast aside like Saul? 'Do not cast me from your presence or take your Holy Spirit from me' (verse 11). Is his life going to end in similar tragedy? Is he going to be passed over? Will God no longer be able to use him as a preacher or a worker? Will God have to stop that work that he has begun? It's too awful a thought for any of us.

But what is so wonderful and unusual in this psalm is that the chief pain in David is not remorse or those superficial things that come to all of us when we sin or do evil; it is the pain of a broken fellowship with God. Is there any other pain greater than to break a relationship with those who are nearest and dearest to us? It's agonizing to be even for a day at cross-purposes with those who are closest to us. We long to put things right; we don't always know how to. Sometimes our stubbornness temporarily makes matters worse, but we long to mend what has been broken. How much more – a thousand times – if the Spirit of God is working, do we want to put back that relationship with God that has been broken?

Verse 12: 'Restore to me the joy of your salvation and grant me a willing spirit, to sustain me.' This was his response to God's revelation, God's light focusing in on his heart and showing him that adultery and murder were not exceptional events for which he was not really responsible but rather a characteristic of the real, deep-down David. He understood that this was the real man, that this was the real heart. It is said that in times of revival this sort of pain and distress, this conviction of sin, precedes conversion. Well – it is so in history, but it doesn't seem to be so in our own day, does it? It is, one must say, very rare before conversion.

Yet we must add that, notwithstanding, conviction of sin must happen. It is one of the peculiar and special works of the Holy Spirit. Sooner or later the joy will disappear, the Holy Spirit will take it away. Sooner or later he will no longer comfort us but cause us acute discomfort. Sooner or later he will cease to minister to us the peace of God and he will begin to destroy our peace. Sooner or later God the Holy Spirit must bring us face to face with the pain of a guilty conscience, the pain of being a thankless rebel. Read Psalm 51 and you will see that David has woken up first to this great revelation of the endemic power of evil, rediscovered in this experience, and that now he has responded to it with unappeasable pain. That pain is something quite new in his life. It is something indispensable to anybody who is going to be a leader, indeed to any Christian at all who wants to know reality.

'Oh,' you say, 'this is a gloomy evening!'

No, cheer up, this is a healthy evening, it's a grand evening! To put aside all pretence, to be on the level with God and one another – what a relief! There's a lot of face-painting in the Christian life – wonderful, cheerful expressions that say, 'Yes, all is well.' But here we're going deeper than that. Let's turn to the second great revelation and the second great response.

God's revelation of the loyalty of a covenant-keeping God

When you are in such despair as this, in the pit, in the far country – there comes a time when you feel you can never face up to God and return at all. How can we go back? We've done it so many times. Our excuses are so feeble. God must see through us. Someone said to me the other day, 'I'm going to do it again, so why do I come back?'

Verse 1 gives us a glorious answer; one not, I think, made quite clear by the English translations. And I want to say that it is one of the great verses of Psalm 51, perhaps even of the Psalter: I believe that the whole psalm would never have been written, but for the knowledge that is revealed in verse 1. If David had not known this truth he wouldn't have dared to put pen to paper, and he wouldn't have dared to go back to God.

There are two realities here in verse 1.

God's unbreakable covenant loyalty and grace

That is what the little phrase 'unfailing love' in line 2 means. And I fear it doesn't get anywhere near the heart of the matter. 'Unfailing love' here means God's covenant loyalty. The glory of being a Christian and a believer, the glory that was within reach of David at this moment, is not that we are committed to him but that he is committed to us. In so many astounding ways this great truth, that God has taken hold of me and will not let me go, is made plain in many wonderful places.

I think of that terrible story in Exodus 32, when Moses comes down from the mountain and finds the golden calf. '"I have seen these people," the LORD said to Moses, "and they are a stiff-necked people. Now leave me alone [let me go] so that my anger may burn against them and that I may destroy them. Then I will make you into a great nation"' (verses 9–10). What is God teaching us by that extraordinary phrase, 'Let me go'? How can Moses have any hold on God?

You will know from Exodus 32 that Moses then pleads with God. He tells him how he has taken these people to himself and how he has sworn to keep them. He reminds God of his covenant loyalty. He tells God of his promises, and God turns aside from his desire and his plan to destroy his people. Of course that does not mean that Moses changed God's mind. What it means is that God is teaching us that when we hold on to him with his promises and covenant loyalty, we will not be destroyed; because he is a God who cannot lie and cannot break his promises. There's nothing sentimental about this. It is the rock on which all Christian living depends. If you want a New Testament reference, the one that comes most often to my mind is Mark 14:24. Breaking bread and pouring wine, Jesus says to this little frightened band of disciples, 'This is my blood of the covenant, which is poured out for many.' And then he tells them, 'You're all going to fall away' (*cf.* verse 27).

Isn't that reality? A covenant is made, and the one who makes the covenant says to the other party, 'Of course you'll break it straight away.' But Jesus adds, 'After I have risen, I will go before you into Galilee, because I will not break it' (*cf.* verse 28).

God's great compassion and tender mercy

There is something else David knows about God that may perhaps be unclear in the translation of verse 1, though this one is a little plainer: 'according to your great compassion'. This is the second thing that makes it possible for David to draw near. He does so without presumption because God is a God of covenant loyalty and a God of tender mercies.

The word here is an emotional one. The same Hebrew word was used of Joseph's heart when he yearned for his brother Benjamin. Do you remember? In that great auditorium where his brothers stood before him, he was so deeply moved that he 'hurried out and looked for a place to weep', then dried his tears and washed his face and came back again. He was deeply moved to see his younger brother restored; deeply moved to see God keeping his promises (cf. Gn. 43:30).

That same emotional yearning is here in verse 1. Why should God have anything to do with David? Why should God have anything to do with you and me? It's not rational. It's according to his covenant loyalty and it's according to his tender mercy. If you can remember those two great 'accordings' you will never be so far away in the pigsty in the far country that you can't come back. There may be somebody here who'll need them one day, who in absolute desperation will open his or her Bible at Psalm 51 and say, 'I have no right to come back, but according to your covenant loyalty and according to your great yearning I come back.'

So in verse 1 there are two revelations. The revelation of his sin led David to a new knowledge of himself, and the revelation of God's covenant loyalty and yearning heart led David to a new knowledge of God. My friends, if your experience of failure leads you to such new knowledge of yourself you will rejoice in the sovereign purposes that have led you.

What, then, is David's response to this second revelation?

David's response of incomparable hope

Look at the cries, the hopes, the new resolutions that now pour out of his mouth. Verse 10, 'Create in me a pure heart.' He's talking to the Creator, the one who brings something out of nothing. He knows that in the depths of his heart is impurity and defilement, so he turns to God and says, 'Create in me a pure heart . . . and renew a steadfast spirit within me.' Verse 12, 'Restore to me the joy of your salvation and grant me a willing spirit, to sustain me.' And how wonderfully the prayer of verse 13 has been answered! Since this psalm was written, David has shown generations of sinners the way home to God long after they thought themselves to be beyond recall.

This is David's response to the revelation of who God is. These insistent cries for help, these new resolutions, are a sign of his incomparable hope. He's not too proud to make resolutions. Verse 14: he is going to sing again. Verse 15: he is going to declare God's praise. Verse 18: he expresses his hopes that as a result of this, God's people are going to be built up, that there's going to be a new hope for them and Jerusalem is going to be built.

Earlier I issued a warning against impetuous and over-optimistic resolutions. But resolutions are not of themselves a bad thing. Sometimes we have too worldly a view on this. We know how quickly our new resolutions will be broken, so we fear it is futile to make them. But the Christian life is one of making new resolutions almost daily. It's a life of incomparable hope, so that it is worth making new resolutions. It is worth trying again.

Who, then, is this worshipper in verse 17? He is a renewed and a restored person. He has been humbled; that means he's simply been brought to an honest and proper place of unpretentious joy and honest confidence in God. He's no longer living a lie. He's happy now to be a sinner saved by grace all his life long, kept by mercy, new every morning. He now knows himself in a new way, and he does not despair. He now knows God in a new way, and is full of incomparable hope.

'The sacrifices of God are a broken spirit; a broken and contrite heart, O God, you will not despise.' Those are his words, not mine. Praise God for them.

4

The great Christ

by Stephen Gaukroger

Colossians 1:15–23

I'm conscious that any words I might add to this great passage could be construed as lessening their impact and obscuring their truth rather than releasing it. Such is the poverty of human words, compared with the written word of God. I'm praying tonight that as we look at this passage together we will become excited again about the Scripture, and particularly about our theme: 'The great Christ.'

What I want to say tonight divides into three sections: the Christ who is *great in his person* (verses 15ff.); the Christ who is *great in his purpose* (verses 20ff.); and the Christ who is *great in his people* (verse 23).

The book of Colossians is addressed to a church in a town that was fairly well past its sell-by date. It used to be influential, powerful, a thriving commercial centre; but at this period in its history Colosse has travelled far down a downward track. The Colossians are a discouraged people, far from their former glory, their days of empire long forgotten and surrounded by towns now much more influential. The church here, with which Paul was very unfamiliar, was probably one of the first church-plants out of the Ephesian church which was a hundred or so miles away. And so to this young church Paul writes a message of encouragement in a town in decline. Not only is the town in decline and therefore probably casting a general air of depression over the people of God who live there; the young church itself is having its lifeblood threatened by a heresy that is like a virulent disease.

It's dangerous because it's subtle. It's not the kind of heresy that denies, for example, the divinity of Jesus or the manhood of Jesus. Something like that would be obvious and easily repelled. This heresy is carefully phrased and delicately insinuated into the life of the church. And as we unpack these verses together, we'll see a little bit of how this heresy came to be influential and how these verses are written to rebut those insinuations. How appropriate that tonight we should be looking at Jesus and attempting to make sure that our understanding of Jesus is soundly orthodox and not letting any of these things creep into our own church life!

For example, one of the characteristics of this particular heresy was that it claimed that Jesus was a very good person. So far, so good. But it claimed that he was only one of a number of intermediaries between human beings and God; that, good though he was, and God though he may have been, he wasn't in himself sufficient for the salvation of the people of God. It was a 'Jesus and' heresy, and part of Paul's purpose is to say to us that there is only one Jesus, who is totally and utterly without peer and is completely sufficient. How we need that word, at the end of the twentieth century in the evangelical church: 'Jesus alone is sufficient.'

Jesus is great in his person

Paul lists four things in this passage which, in terms of the person of Christ, outline his greatness. The first is in verse 15: 'He is *the image of the invisible God* . . .'

This means that Jesus is not simply a representation of God (like a picture, or an image on a coin, or a photograph or artist's drawing), but that he is a manifestation of God. He *is* God. Throughout these four initial points you'll almost hear Paul breathing in the background, '. . . And there is no-one else like this.' Whatever other intermediaries you talk of, what powers you call on, what other spirit beings (demonic or angelic) you believe exist between God and man, Paul says, Jesus is the only one in all creation who is the manifestation of the living God.

For converts from Judaism (and there would have been some in Colosse), it would have been an awesome reminder. They would have been staggered to realize that the Yahweh they had known all their lives had an image on earth. For the orthodox, traditional Jew, that was almost blasphemy. Yet Paul does not shrink from claiming it. The one who said that he was the I AM is the manifestation of God. If you want to know what God is like, look at Jesus.

And Paul goes on to say that he's not only the image of the invisible God, but he is *the firstborn over all creation*. In the fourth century by the Arians and in the twentieth century by the Jehovah's Witnesses, this verse has continued to be abused and twisted to mean that Jesus one of the created order, rather than its author. But the verse cannot mean that. 'Firstborn' means first in terms of priority of time and rank. Jesus is the eternal Son of God, and 'firstborn' means 'from the beginning with the Father'. God is eternally Father; and in order for him to be eternally Father, he needs from eternity to have had a Son.

Seven years ago I became a father, but I have not always been a father. There was a point when I wasn't a father. I was a father only when I had a child, but God has always been a Father, and he always has to have had a Son. So the eternal Father and the eternal Son have been together for ever, and this God is the firstborn over all creation. And Paul whispers again: 'There's no-one like that either! You talk to me of your intermediaries, the other powers you call on; but there's no-one apart from Jesus in this category.'

He continues, *by him all things were created*. The phrase 'all things' occurs twice in verse 16, deliberately repeated to remind us that there isn't anything outside the created power of Jesus Christ – none of these intermediary forces, nothing you can see, nothing you can't see, nothing you can imagine, nothing from the past, nothing from the present, nothing in the future; nothing is outside the scope of his creation. Paul is saying that if these intermediaries exist at all, they are not the colleagues of Jesus. They are part of his creation, and they owe it all to him. He is the great creator God. John 1:3 picks up the theme: 'Through him all things were made; without him nothing was made that has been made.' All that you see around you is made by this Jesus. 'And there is no-one else like this.'

'*He is before all things*, and in him all things hold together.'

Verse 17 is a kind of summary of this part of the passage. He holds all things together; they cohere in him; he is the great co-ordinator of everything. Everything exists for his pleasure. The beauty of creation, the glory of all we see; every person made, every thing made; it was made for the pleasure of Jesus. No other spirit being can come anywhere close to claiming this. What an amazing thing it is, that all of our universe comes together, coheres and finds its order and purpose in him! We do not see that in our universe. It all appears chaotic to us. But because Jesus is the controller, even though we see chaos we actually have a cosmos, an order which is in place because of his power. William Hendriksen, commenting on this passage in his Banner of Truth commentary on Colossians, says this:

> Often confusion seems to be rampant. A guiding hand is nowhere visible. Instead we hear the cry of battle, the shriek of anguish. The newspapers are filled with accounts of burglary, murder, rape and race clash. All is chaos now. But is it really? Should we not rather compare our world to a weaving whose underside forms no intelligible pattern, but whose upperside reveals beauty and design?

How many of us here feel in a state of confusion? How unreal it seems that all things cohere in Christ, or find their order in him! How far from the truth it seems! And yet with the eye of faith we see beyond the chaos, to the order that is hidden and will one day in Christ be revealed.

> My life is but a weaving between my Lord and me.
> I cannot choose the colours he worketh steadily.
> Oft times he weaveth sorrow, and I in foolish pride
> Forget he sees the upper and I the underside.
> The dark threads are as needful in the weaver's skilful hand
> As the threads of gold and silver in the pattern he has planned.

Not till the loom is silent and the shuttles cease to fly,
Shall God unroll the canvas and explain the reason why.

(Anon.)

Let this verse 17 be a comfort to you. Though all seems in confusion in your life, your home and your church; though all seems in chaotic confusion in your world, there is one who stands above it all and whose order will at the end of time be revealed to have been clear. And he will be revealed to have been in control from the beginning. Though we do not see that purpose now, we will see it then.

So Christ is great in his person; there is no-one else like him. And those truths about the greatness of the Christ we serve are a challenge to the pluralism of our age, where tolerance is the key to everything. My brothers and sisters, there is one principle at least that is greater than tolerance, and that is truth. The church of Jesus must never forsake this truth that Jesus is the great Christ, than whom none is greater. He is not one product among many in the religious supermarket for folk to pick and choose as they will; he is the soul's only mediator between God and man. He is the man, Christ Jesus. There is no other Saviour, there never will be, and the church must proclaim the glorious greatness of the Christ we have. We are immensely privileged to have this kind of Saviour.

But not only do these verses challenge the pluralism of our age, but, brothers and sisters, more personally, they challenge the pluralism of our hearts. Herbert Carson, writing on this passage in his Tyndale Commentary on Colossians, says, 'Jesus must be Lord in the lives of his own with a sovereignty which brooks no rival.' If Jesus is all these things, he is a great Christ, great in his person. The call of Scripture is for us to acknowledge that, not simply with our lips but in our lives. His lordship must not be simply something we trip off our tongues but something in which we allow the Scripture to change our very beings. Is Jesus genuinely this Lord in our lives? Or is our head knowledge all we have of this glorious lordship?

Jesus is great in his purpose

Do you see how, in verse 18, Paul is keen not to let his adversaries off the hook? He's anxious to say that this Christ isn't simply great as a distant person, but that he is exercising his authority. 'And he is the head of the body, the church . . . .' Paul, of course, has already used the image of headship and the image of the body in Corinthians, where he talks about the head as the controlling agent of the body below it, sending out commands and controls to the various limbs and extremities in order that they may move at the head's bidding.

Jesus is the head of the church. We ought to pause for a moment to say that that stark, simple phrase to the church at Colosse reminds every pastor and every leader that the church is not ours to control or dispose of as we will. Sometimes I hear ministers talking about 'my church' and 'my people' in a way which speaks of ownership and is unhelpful. Of course loyalty is good and right; of course there must be commitment. But, brothers and sisters, it is the church of Jesus. And there are times when I believe he is asking for it back; that he wants to have the church for which he gave his life because he is its head. He's not a titular head. Jesus is no constitutional monarch; he is a dictator. And sometimes in our easy-going, constitutional monarchy we forget it.

Jesus is not open to be balloted. Sometimes, for example, our understanding of God and his laws is a little like a history exam. 'The Ten Commandments: attempt any three out of ten.' But it's not a multiple choice. In dealing with Jesus we can't pick and choose and hope to get a better deal. He is the head of the church, and that means that all pastors, leaders and church members must submit their prejudices, dreams for their local church and their desires for it to Christ's lordship. If we don't, we are actually saying our view of the church is more important than his.

His lordship is expressed, you will see, in the fact that he is *the beginning and the firstborn* (there's that phrase again) *from among the dead.* Of course Jesus wasn't the first person to come alive from death. One only has to think of the widow of Nain's son and of Lazarus as two classic New Testament examples. So we are obviously not talking of mere resuscitation. We are talking here about coming alive, never to die. No wonder the gates of hell won't prevail against this person's church; he has defeated death and Satan and hell by being the firstborn from the resurrection; the very first to be alive for evermore.

'The beginning' – notice, he's the originator. The church is God's idea. It's worth remembering that, when you're particularly disillusioned with your own local church. Jesus is the author, the beginning of the church. He originated it and he is the leader of it, the first of those who would rise from death and never, never die. What a thrilling thought! This is the purpose of God in Christ. No wonder we've got a great Christ and a lot to shout about. In a few days' time, at Easter, we're going to celebrate that Jesus is alive, risen from the dead, the firstborn of all creation.

There have been hundreds of movements throughout human history. Marx is dead. Ghandi is dead. Muhammad is dead. But Jesus is alive! He is the firstborn from the dead. What a thrilling thing! I go out with confidence in evangelism; I go into praise with confidence; I go into fellowship with confidence, because I don't worship a dead Saviour. His body isn't rotting in some Galilean hillside. The leader of our church is not dead but is alive.

And more than that. Marvel at this: *God was pleased to have all his fullness dwell in him* (verse 19). The word for 'fullness' is used almost twenty times in the New Testament, but only four times in this particular sense, that the fullness of God is in Christ. It's an interesting word, sometimes used of a ship's complement, the complete number being made up; or of the inhabitants of a town or city when a census is taken. It's the total, added up, with no-one missing. In Jesus we have the total of God with nothing missing. We don't have a bit of him, we don't have a toned-down version or a pale reflection or a second-division kind of God. We have all of God in this Jesus.

That is important, for he has to do an amazing task.

Verse 20: 'And through him to reconcile to himself all things, whether things on earth or things in heaven, by making peace through his blood, shed on the cross.' The purpose of this great Christ is not simply to be filled with the fullness of God, to be the originator of the church and its head, but also to reconcile to himself all those who are enemies to himself. Romans 5:1–11 picks up this theme. We were enemies; we were helpless; we were in rebellion against him. But he has broken down that wall of partition and made it possible for reconciliation to take place.

How can we ever forget those scenes on our television screens when men and women with their bare hands hacked away at the Berlin Wall and finally bulldozed it down. East joined West; the divide was gone. Brothers and sisters, a far greater wall was dividing us from God. And he, in the person of Jesus, tore it down, and as he tore it down his hands were bleeding. But he died in order to tear it down, so that all my enmity with him, the fact that I was out of fellowship with God, was now forgotten and forgiven and dealt with through his all-sufficient sacrifice. And now I am in relationship with him; I am right with him; I am reconciled to him. What an amazing message!

The implication is of course that as I am reconciled to God I can be reconciled to my brother and sister in Christ. Isn't that where much of the reconciliation conversations in the world are going so badly wrong? Jesus is simply left out of the equation. Television has turned the world into a neighbourhood, but only God through Christ can turn it into a brotherhood. There is no other way. Reconciliation between black and white, between different racial groupings, between the ethnic groupings of the former Yugoslavia or wherever, can ultimately be reconciled only when Jesus is in the picture. It can only be as we are reconciled vertically with this God that there is any possibility of deep reconciliation with others; the reconciliation bought through the blood of God's Son.

Verse 21 continues: 'Once you were alienated from God and were enemies in your minds because of your evil behaviour.' One of the lovely things about Paul is that he doesn't mince his words. This is blunt speaking. There's no anaesthetic in this verse to make it easier or more palatable. You were like aliens on another planet as far as God was concerned; far away, enemies in your mind. Why? Because of your evil behaviour.

Now note this: the Colossian heresy ridiculed the idea of evil behaviour. The body, and matter itself, were things we could safely ignore. Spirituality was all 'up there'. It was a relationship on the level of feeling; a spirituality, an attitude. It certainly had nothing to do with behaviour. All kinds of immorality were being tolerated in Colosse. And something of this insipid doctrine was getting into the church.

So Paul does not hesitate to condemn evil behaviour for what it is and call the Colossian church to repentance. 'This is why Christ died,' he says, 'in order for you to recognize how bad you are, then he could put it right.'

The greatest problem in saving a drowning person comes when the drowning person tries to save himself. The belief that he can help in the rescue process contributes sometimes to the untimely death of both the drowner and the rescuer. It's not until the drowning person abandons hope that he can ultimately be rescued. And, brothers and sisters, it's not until we recognize there is no good thing in us that we can hope for the help of the living God. That's challenging; it hurts our ego; it challenges our pride. But without that understanding, there is no hope in God. We need to challenge that easy-believism which says, 'Just come to God as you are. He wants to bless you' – as if there were no cost or recognition of our sinfulness involved. The Bible is utterly clear that without Christ we are alienated from God, lost in evil behaviour and enemies of him. And we need to be made holy.

Look what he's done (verse 22). He has reconciled us by this death we've spoken about, to do three things: to present us holy, to present us without blemish, and to present us free from accusation. 'Holiness' talks about separation from sin and how we receive that blessing from God. 'Without blemish' refers to the sacrificial system: we do not offer a lamb that's dirty or diseased or imperfect, but one without blemish; so we are presented to God without spot, and free from accusation. What glorious release that is! God won't accuse us; Satan can't accuse us, and we mustn't accuse ourselves. That's what God has done for us in Christ.

And so as we read that the purpose of this great Christ is reconciliation and to make us holy, it suddenly dawns on us that holy living is not an optional extra for the believer. It's part and parcel of what we were born again for, part and parcel of the purpose of the gospel message. It finally dawns on us that we've got to stop our sexually immoral behaviour; we've got to stop cheating the tax man; we've got to stop gossiping. And we've got to start giving generously to God's work; we've got to start working hard at studying the Scripture; not simply because he commands those things, but because the very purpose for which Jesus died was to make us holy, and when we are not holy our lives deny the crucifixion and the resurrection itself.

And so the word tonight is not to induce guilt, to urge us to sort things out because otherwise God will be angry with us, but to show us that inherent in the message of salvation is the truth that God is a holy God. And he has called us to be holy and it was his purpose from the beginning to make us holy, and we want to live in glorious joy to be like our Father.

Jesus is great in his people

'If you continue in your faith . . . .' Verse 23 is a call to perseverance in the light of complacency. It's not really a test verse for the debate over whether faith can be lost. Thankfully, I shan't be addressing that subject this evening.

F. F. Bruce, commenting on this verse, says: 'If the Bible teaches the final perseverance of the saints, it also teaches that the saints are those who finally persevere.' Continuance is the test of reality. John Calvin observes of this passage: 'The writer intimates that we are only *en route* and we have not reached our goal. Our faith is not to be like a mere opinion which is shaken by various movements, but has a firm steadfastness able to withstand all the machinations of hell itself.' This is a call to go on going on. Or, in the words of Winston Churchill to a nation at war, 'Never, never, never give up.'

There was a danger, Paul felt, that the Colossians might be tempted to believe that Jesus was so great, and had done so much that was wonderful, that they could forget it all now and just leave it to him. Let him get on with it; let him be this marvellous, great person with this wonderful purpose. But no, says Paul, not a bit of it. 'You must be', as he says in 2 Corinthians, 'co-workers with this great God. Just because he's sovereign you cannot abdicate responsibility for playing your part in responding to this' (*cf.* 2 Cor. 6:1). So you must continue in your faith. Do not be complacent. Go on going on.

'Established and firm, not moved . . . .' This is a most unusual word in the original Greek. The Lycus Valley, where Colosse was built, was noted for its earthquakes. In fact one early writer described the Lycus Valley as, in modern parlance, 'earthquake-friendly': that's the exact translation of the Greek word he used. There were regular tremors. And the word for 'tremor' lies behind this word 'moved'. You must be not shaken when the earthquake comes.

It was a familiar picture. Colossian homes were probably shaken regularly. The people would know what it meant to grasp bits of furniture to stopping them falling over. It reminded them of how easy it was to be moved. Their whole homes, in fact, may have been moved. But the writer says, 'You must not be moved.' Go on going on, continuing in your most holy faith.

For those of you here tonight who are struggling desperately with the Christian faith, this is a message of hope. It's not simply a whip to beat us – 'Go on going on even though you don't feel like it.' It's a reminder that because our Christ is great in his person, because he is great in his purpose, he is already working in you the work of perseverance. He is working that work out already, and your work of continuing is in partnership with him. You're not on your own as you work it out.

And God is not unaware tonight of the earthquakes going on in this room, the earthquakes in your life. He knows that some of you are facing the spectre of unemployment, that there are strains and tensions in some of our marriages, that there's financial stress and pressure in many households at this time. These earthquakes do not contradict our faith; and as we recognize that we're in Christ, they do not shake it – because we persist with the one who persists with us, inside us; the great perseverer with the saints.

Paul closes this whole passage, not just in a call to perseverance but in a call to acknowledge the spread of the gospel. What does Jesus do in his people? He encourages them to go on and also he encourages them that the gospel is being spread. 'This is the gospel that you heard.' Don't go after some other gospel you've only just heard. Remember the gospel you heard in the beginning, the original gospel. Don't give way to these cunning and deceitful fables that you hear.

And listen to this! Even allowing for a little Pauline exaggeration, this is an amazing claim: 'and that has been proclaimed to every creature under heaven'. All the world is aware that Jesus Christ is Lord. All the world is continuing to be made aware of it, from that point down the centuries to this. And again Paul draws on the background of the heresy into which he preaches. The Colossian heresy was selective, specialized and elitist. There were certain people with special knowledge; if you were in the 'in crowd' you could find out about it, but if not, it wasn't for you. It was for an elite, the privileged few. But Paul is at pains to point out that this is the gospel for the world.

Oh, they'll not all believe. They'll not all respond. They'll not all receive. But the world is open to this message. No favourites: to all of us, ignorant, intelligent, black, white, slave, free, cultured, uncultured, from any background, the gospel message comes.

Notice, too, the contrast. I think it's probably deliberate that Paul mentions his own name here: 'of which I, Paul, have become a servant'. He is contrasting the grandeur and splendour of the gospel with the insignificance of the messenger. 'Paul' means 'little' or 'small'. And here Paul doesn't describe himself as an ambassador but as a servant, a slave.

He minimizes himself and pours glory on the gospel of God.

Now, isn't that a wonderful example to us? The glory is all this great Christ's, not mine. It's his gospel, it's his church. Everything we've said tonight has pointed away from man and to Jesus himself. Paul, little Paul, mere servant of this great God, has been given the immense privilege of taking the gospel of reconciliation to the whole world.

How easy it is, you know, after a week like this, to be incredibly arrogant about what we have learnt. There are members of your church family who are dreading your return! They're sure you're going to come back from Word Alive fired up, thrilled, blessed, educated, knowing so much about Malachi. They can't even find the book in the Old Testament! And so we go back from an event like this with a kind of fake spirituality, a pseudo-godly air, walking back into our home churches this Easter Sunday with our noses in the air spiritually: 'I've been to the Mount.' You haven't, you've been to Butlin's! It is critical to understand this. The honour and glory of the gospel lie not in what I have learnt this week, what I am gaining, what I have got in my possession, what I am in Christ. It's little Paul, the servant, compared with the glorious riches of the gospel of reconciliation taken into all the world.

And I pray, brothers and sisters, as you and I go back into our world, our homes, our churches, our schools, our universities, our streets and our towns with this gospel of reconciliation, we will go back not to exalt ourselves but to exalt Jesus; not to talk about us but to talk about him, and to remind ourselves that the news which was good news in the ancient world, which brought together men and women from every background and reconciled them to God, is still available today. And I pray that we will go back with this good news ringing in our ears: 'We are weak but he is strong.'

We have a Christ who is great in his person, great in his purpose and great in his people. No wonder we're thrilled to be known as 'Christ-ians' – Christians, going back to love and serve and win a world for this great Christ.

5

The great hope

by Philip Hacking

I Peter 1:1–12

It has been a great joy to be here this week. There is a sense in which the magnificent theme of 'hope' is particularly appropriate to this last evening; for all of us who have been involved in this project since its beginning have had some trepidation and a lot of faith. And faith has been rewarded; this has been a memorable week.

Roy Clements has reminded us of the cynicism prevalent in Malachi's time, and related it to the very cynical world in which we live. 'We live', he told us, 'in a world that has lost its hope.' I believe that to be profoundly true. And it is a tremendous challenge to us. For what a great opportunity we have! There is no other hope. The world is bankrupt.

On a deeply distressing television programme about sex and teenagers, I saw a group talking about their sexual experiences. When they had all finished, a lass of fourteen simply said, 'I wish somebody would tell us what is right and what is wrong.' In such situations, if we believe the hope, we have a tremendous opportunity.

I remember leading a mission twenty years ago at Leicester University where there was great opposition from the Humanist Society (actually they were a tremendous help: there's nothing like great opposition to bring the crowds!). They had a message and a hope, and they opposed ours. Those were eventful, stirring days. But they've gone. The Communists, too, had a message and a hope – but the Communist empires have gone and the hope has gone.

Yet for us the hope is still there.

If it were not for the fact that it would ruin the week's list of titles, I would call this talk not 'The Great Hope' but 'What a Hope!' Because that, I believe, is what the world is saying today, cynically assuming that what is hoped for will never happen. But it is what we say too, though with a different emphasis. I would love to think that we will go out from here to live as enthusiastically as we have sung, to commend Jesus as enthusiastically as we have praised him.

There is a sense in which 'hope' can mean mere wishful thinking. It is the kind of hope that hopes that a favourite football team will win the Cup. Sometimes that wishful thinking, which can never be sure, proves to be justified and what is hoped for happens. But I want to contrast this tenuous hope with a hope that is gloriously sure. For the world honestly believes that we – with our tremendous hope, to which I draw your attention in 1 Peter this evening – are just as hopeless as they are.

Peter's testimony

So let's take these twelve verses. Peter is probably writing in AD 63. He is writing to a church that's beginning to be persecuted. Yet I don't think it's obvious from these early verses. You may have spotted 'grief in all kinds of trials . . . refined by fire' (verses 6–7), but Peter's main thrust is praise.

In the first three verses the full name of Jesus comes four times. Peter wisely starts not with the troubles of the world, nor with the coming persecution, but with the glory of Jesus. I do hope that when we as Christians go out into a world that grumbles about hopelessness, we speak of Jesus. We're all so self-centred – the kind of people who when asked 'How are you?' are still telling you forty-five minutes later. But the world means not only 'How are you?' but 'What sort of Saviour have you got?'

Peter is writing thirty years after he first preached the gospel on the day of Pentecost. I always remember that story because I was once asked to take the role of Peter in a dramatic performance at my church in Sheffield. I had to preach his Pentecost sermon. I wasn't allowed a Bible or notes, and for obvious reasons I wasn't allowed to quote from the writings of Paul! It was a moving experience for me, as I actually prepared to give, not my own sermon, but Peter's. I found it remarkable to imagine Peter's thoughts. 'How is it that I am speaking to thousands of people with courage and conviction when six weeks ago, almost on this very spot, I couldn't admit to a little lass that I was a follower of Jesus? What's happened to me?'

Two things had happened to him. One, he'd discovered the risen Jesus. Two, the Spirit of God had come upon him and consequently he had that tremendous conviction. Now, those things have happened to us. So we should be able to go out with the same confidence as Peter. Thirty years on, and he's still as sure as ever! One of the great things about Word Alive is that all ages are here. It's great to see the young people and students here. But many of us are older. I wonder if our courage, conviction and enthusiasm are as great? Do we still have the passion that Roy spoke of in his Malachi studies, which is so often lacking in our churches? Here is Peter thirty years on, as keen as ever.

Peter's readers

He's writing to Christians who are *scattered* (verse 1). We too are going to be scattered tomorrow, some of us back to churches alive and vigorous, some of us to places desperately needy. And if Word Alive is what it claims to be, then that word will be alive through us. Please, don't go back merely talking about the excitement of Spring Harvest – some ministers and friends are afraid when people come back from big conventions. But go back with a renewed love and conviction.

Where were they scattered? Well, you can read the names in verse 1: Pontus, Galatia, Cappadocia, Asia and Bithynia. These were very wealthy areas culturally and financially, but spiritually they were poverty-stricken. They had plenty of religion. You could take your pick of any religion you liked. There were Greek gods, mystery cults, Stoicism, nihilist religions, emperor worship and the Jewish faith. There were the best of religions to be found there – but they were still imperfect.

And in that world of hopelessness, here are Christians about to be persecuted; and Peter tells them what a great hope they have.

Our nation is not irreligious, but it's hopeless. Oh, there's the pick of religions to be had, more and more of them; but men and women need to know from scattered Christians what the true message is.

They're not only scattered, but (verse 1) they're *strangers*. They don't belong there. We meet here in Butlin's, but I'm glad to be going home tomorrow. We've been well served by our friends at Butlin's, it's been great and we thank God for them. But nevertheless, this is a passing place. We are strangers here. And what we have to get across to men and women as Christians is that we belong to the world in one sense, but in another, we don't. We're not meant to be weird and peculiar, people without their feet on the ground who can't talk in everyday language. Yet if there's no difference between us and the world, if we are bounded by this world's horizons, then we fail our Saviour.

I suggest that in these verses there are three glorious tenses of the Christian hope. Hold on to them, believe them to be true, let God speak through them to your heart, so that you will go out to be hopeful and hope-sharing – able, as Peter says (1 Pet. 3:15), to give the reason for your hope.

A hope anchored in the past

It is a hope anchored in the past: and this hope has firstly to do with God.

The Father's work

Yesterday we had a student seminar on predestination. We had a great time and I enjoyed the questions and the debate. Predestination, in its biblical sense, is a glorious truth. It becomes a problem only when people mangle the doctrine at a human level. I know of one extremely reformed group whom I shall not name. I once asked a friend how he would characterize them. He said, quite lovingly, 'Well, you see, their problem is that they're not sure they're going to heaven, but they're *quite* sure no-one else is.' That was probably a bit unfair, but it does express one kind of extreme doctrine of election.

But I find here that my hope does not lie in the fact that I believe in a doctrine called 'predestination', or that I can answer all the students' questions about how to balance predestination and free will. But what I do thank God for is that my salvation is anchored not in my decision, or in the reality of my choice, or in my zeal or in my faith – but in his work. He's chosen us. Jesus said, 'You did not choose me, but I chose you' (Jn. 15:16). It's anchored in the absolute certainty of the Father's work. Paul reminds us in Ephesians and Romans that we are chosen to be holy, we are chosen to be conformed to the likeness of his Son. So you and I have a hope anchored deep in the Father's work.

Secondly, it has to do with Jesus Christ.

The Son's work

When verse 2 speaks of 'sprinkling by his blood', we're back to Calvary and beyond Calvary to the Old Testament, where at Sinai the people of God and the altar were sprinkled with blood as a mark that they were joined in that great covenant of blood. It's a reminder to us that Calvary stands as the historical certainty: God loves us. How tremendous that is! I was very moved, when Roy began his studies in Malachi, by that reminder of God's covenant love. It is not so much the quality of our love, but the certainty of his; and if Malachi could believe it the far side of Calvary, then 'he who did not spare his own Son, but gave him up for us all – how will he not also, along with him, graciously give us all things?' (Rom. 8:32). Because his blood was shed and sprinkled in that covenant way, you and I can be sure both that we have eternal life and that God's love is always with us.

So when I'm troubled as to how I can believe God's love in what is happening in the world and in my life, I look to the cross, which remains a historical fact and a great assurance. The mark of heaven is this: 'A great multitude that no-one could count, from every nation . . . . "These are they who have . . . washed their robes and made them white in the blood of the Lamb"' (Rev. 7:9, 14).

It is a privilege to travel abroad and glimpse the people of God in many parts of the world. I've come back recently from ministering in Japan, and it was very moving to meet the people of God in that land and realize there was a time when we were at enmity with each other. There was a lovely man called John who interpreted for me. I discovered that John's father was killed in the Second World War. I thought, what a strange mystery: his father could have been killed fighting my father, and here we are now preaching Jesus, covered as one in the blood of the Lamb. A few years ago when the Berlin Wall came down we thought Europe was free. But we have opened up a can of worms. It is man against man and people fighting and slaying and raping their neighbours. But *people can be one*. It is a message of hope – it's coming from nowhere else: 'sprinkled by the blood'.

Christ's work means not only being sprinkled by his blood, but also (verse 3) being given 'new birth into a living hope through the resurrection of Jesus Christ from the dead' – literally, 'out of dead men'.

It's a historical resurrection. I look forward to Easter day, when many of us here will be proclaiming the wonder of Jesus risen. I told you earlier how I once took the role of Peter. It was lovely to say, 'God has raised this Jesus' (Acts 2:32). Peter preached it to people who could have walked down the road to the tomb; if he'd been telling a lie, they could have produced the body. This was no myth, no springtime fancy of resurrection. It was historical fact. Paul says, 'If this is not true then our faith is vain, we are to be pitied' (*cf.* 1 Cor. 15:17, 19). Whatever denomination you belong to, when you go back to your church dare to stand for this. We've a battle on our hands in many of our churches. Stand up and be counted – you believe! It's one thing to sing it with hundreds of other people, but it's another to dare to say it when your friends cynically smile at you even in the church.

Sir Norman Anderson, who has been with us briefly this week, has written on both the evidence for the resurrection and the evidence for the historicity of Jesus. Sir Norman was travelling to give a televised broadcast in Scotland on the subject of the Easter resurrection, shortly after his son had died of cancer in his twenties. They offered to cancel his participation in the circumstances, for you can't speak about the resurrection when you've just lost a son. But he said, 'I want to speak about it now even more.' Thank God for people like that. He grasped the truth. When the chips were down and the pressure came to him and his family, he knew it.

Please don't wait until you have to face it in actual experience. Be sure of the truth, and the truth will garrison your heart. He is risen! And it's not just for Easter day. Every time I preach on Easter Day, I end my sermon with the same four words: 'After Easter, always Easter!' We celebrate on Easter Day, but every Lord's day is Easter Day, because he is risen. That's where our hope is. You see, people face this solemn fact of death with absolute certainty. Even in our technological world, you who visit people who are in the shadow of death or recently bereaved know how hopeless people can be. And only we have a hope to share.

The Spirit's work

In verses 10–12 we have a reminder that the Spirit of God has been at work in Scripture. He has given us the word of God. That's why we launched Word Alive; we believe that the word of God is what it says it is, and from the beginning our theme has been that of a God-breathed, God-inspired Scripture. Consequently our faith is anchored not in human ideas, nor in the new things that come from time to time in the life of the church, but in God's authentic Spirit-inspired word.

In verses 2 and 3 we find that through the word of God and the Spirit of God we receive new birth into a living hope. But at the end of the chapter (verse 23) we are born again 'through the living and enduring word of God'. Always word and Spirit together, from Genesis right through to Revelation. Never divorce them. You're born again by the word of God; you are born again by the Spirit of God.

A lady once asked me, when I was visiting in the parish, 'Who are these "born again" people?'

'Oh,' I said, quite straightforwardly, 'I'm one.'

'No,' she said. 'You can't be, you're an Anglican.'

She wasn't being rude. So far as she was concerned you were Anglican, Methodist, Roman Catholic, Baptist or the peculiar people she'd heard about – Born Again. I want to say that if you or I have known that experience of new birth, if it is anchored in the past, in our experience, then it ought to be true of us that we demonstrate in the world the difference that God can make in a human life.

Roy reminded us through Malachi (or Malachi through Roy) that we live in a cynical world. The world is cynical about religious experiences. They're not particularly impressed if you go back and say, 'There were so many people at Word Alive, and it was great to be singing together' – that doesn't impress them. They are very dubious about people who talk about religious experience. But what they cannot gainsay is the reality of a life which is clearly changed and transformed, the power of a born-again child of God.

A hope assured in the future

In these verses we also find two things in the future: the promised land (verse 4) and the promised day (verses 5 and 7).

The promised land

Roy reminded us this morning that we no longer dream. You remember that deeply moving speech of Martin Luther King – 'I have a dream.' Sadly, because so often our dreams have come to nothing, we dare not dream any more, we dare not have visions any more. But I hope you believe there is a promised land waiting for us, 'an inheritance that can never perish, spoil or fade – kept in heaven for you' (verse 4). Please, don't be ashamed of talking about heaven. There is a sense in which that reward is needed. When in the book of Revelation they sang the Hallelujah Chorus, it wasn't just about the glory of heaven, it was also about the downfall of Babylon. It was, as it were, a reminder that God is righteous and just. Hallelujah! In this world the reward will never fully be ours, but there's an inheritance kept safe, secure.

We have been burgled twice. I'll always remember the

first time. They'd left a mess behind. My wife and I went through the gamut of emotions. Our first emotion was anger – fair enough. Our second emotion was to feel upset. Our third emotion (and though we're Christians, we're not particularly 'pious' people) was that we sank to our knees and said 'Thank you' to God out of the depth of our hearts. Not because we had been robbed, but because we realized that the things that had gone, their financial and sentimental worth, were of no real significance. In an odd way, it took something like that to tell us how little importance these things really had. Our insurance company paid up in due course and that helped, but we didn't know that was going to be the case when we said 'Thank you'.

I want to say to you, what the world *does* understand is this kind of thing. How much importance do you really place upon material possessions? We Christians talk very easily about treasure in heaven, where moth and rust don't corrupt and thieves don't break through and steal; but very many of us live as if our treasure were on earth. Are we all that different from our non-Christian neighbours when it comes to what we do with our money, when it comes to security?

One of my congregation was telling me about the testimony he's been able to have, very humbly, in his redundancy. He doesn't like being redundant, but he's found that many of his non-Christian friends believe that there is nothing, they are in despair. And he can talk about a purposeful life. Indeed, he's a tremendously purposeful man. He's accepted that God can use him in his redundancy.

And there is something more important even than that; the promised land. Please hold on to heaven! Believe in it, it's safe, it's secure. The inheritance in the Old Testament was Canaan, and that was often spoiled, fading, and perishing. But heaven is safe. Nothing else is, till then.

The promised day

In verses 5 and 7 we are given that lovely picture of the day when Jesus Christ is revealed. Perhaps this week we have not been able to speak enough about the second coming, that glorious day to which we look. But, and I believe we must get this across, there is one day that we know is certain in the history of the world. We do not know what will happen to people and nations. I fear very much, if I'm honest, for my grandchildren's world. Who knows? I find the world a more threatening place than it was ten years ago, not a less threatening one. And I don't know whether or not we shall see in our own nation a swing back by the grace of God to the ways of Christ. I pray so. I long for revival. But I don't know.

What I *do* know is that Christ returns; when, we know not. Please don't desecrate this great doctrine by trying to attach times and seasons to it. The tragedy is, we've often pushed the doctrine out of the church because extremists have done such despite to its glorious truth. But one day Jesus Christ will be revealed, one day he is coming again. We move towards the dawn.

A hope available in the present

Two little phrases in verse 5 sum it up: 'by God's power' and 'through faith'.

By God's power

God's power is doing two things. In verse 2, God's power is 'sanctifying'; that's the great work of the Spirit – making us holy. That has been our message at Keswick over many years. But holiness is a theme that has been desperately neglected, and the work of the Spirit in our hearts is primarily a work of sanctifying us, of making us like Jesus. So we go out from here with this tremendous hope: we're not just waiting for heaven.

I'm not – to coin a phrase – 'dying to go to heaven'. I can't say that at this moment I am waiting and wishing that tomorrow I could be there. I've got a job on earth to do. Maybe I'm not holy enough yet. I long to see, in the days the Lord still gives me, myself becoming a little more worthy of my Lord and Saviour. There's a lot of work still to do in my life and in yours, but how good that he's still working the sanctifying work of the Spirit!

But the other work of God's power is seen in verse 5: we are being shielded by God's power. That word 'shielded' is used in Philippians 4:7 – 'The peace of God, which transcends all understanding, will guard your hearts and your minds.' It's a military word. We are being kept, guarded, protected.

That does not mean we are immune from trouble, that we shall have no suffering. It does not mean that we shall prosper in materialistic terms. Of course it doesn't! May we get hold of the fact that God, in his infinite mercy and wisdom, allows suffering and works through it. Peter points out in verses 6 and 7 that you are going to be tested; and that's good, because you matter, and we expect that we should be tested, and we are being kept in the midst of testing.

A few years ago I was well off enough to buy my first new car. I'd driven – as all good ministers should! – second-hand cars for a long time. Now I'd saved up enough for a new car. The gentleman selling it to me knew me. He was busy explaining how they always put any new model of a car through all the tests that could be devised. Then he gave me a peculiar look and said, 'Of course, some people drive in such a way that we haven't thought of a test that can possibly cover it . . . .' Which is rather unfair! But he was pointing out that they tried to put new models through every test, because they wanted them to be able to stick to the road.

Don't you expect that God will test you?

And dare you pray to go out from these lovely days together, into the world, not to be kept secure, but to be a witness whatever happens? When the early Christians in Acts 4 began to be persecuted, this same Peter stood with John before the Sanhedrin. Afterwards they went back to the prayer meeting. How did they pray? Not 'Please, Lord keep us safe; please, Lord, take this persecution away.' No! They prayed, 'Give us boldness to preach and do miracles and signs through your name, the name of Jesus' (*cf.* Acts 4:29–30).

Oh, I long for that truly militant Christianity which dares

to say to God, 'I don't just want to be protected, I don't just want an easy life, I want boldness to preach; and if by your grace that means that I'm going to go through days of testing and preach in those days – then, God, give me grace to be bold.'

And oddly enough I believe the world will sit up and take notice, when they see Christians who are not soft, Christians with backbone and fibre who make it quite clear that this is something worth living for and dying for. That is the kind of hope into which we go. God's power will shield us. He'll protect us, he'll keep us till that day.

The Bible does *not* say that he will not allow us even to die in persecution. I remember a moment at a missionary meeting which I happened to be chairing many years ago in Edinburgh. There had been the troubles in the Congo (now Zaire). A couple who had come back from there gave their testimony, saying how people had prayed for God's protection for them and he had brought them out. We were all moved.

Then a little lady raised her hand and asked if she could say something. She came to the front, and very tentatively said: 'I want you to know that my son was killed out in the Congo. We prayed very much for him, and we actually believe that our prayers were answered because we know that his death has been the means of other people coming to Christ.' It was a most moving moment. Of course the couple who had been delivered were only too pleased to agree that yes, that was also true.

They prayed in Acts and this same Peter was brought out of prison. They prayed in Acts and James was martyred. There is no suggestion that if only they'd prayed more, James wouldn't have been martyred.

Some years ago, when I first went to Africa, I stood in a little graveyard in the north of Nigeria. What touched me was not only the graves of the missionaries, but those of their families, their children who died, when the gospel first went out to that country that was then so dangerously unhealthy for Europeans to live in. And I could hear down below in the valley a church packed with young Nigerians singing God's praise.

The blood of the martyrs is the seed of the church. Good Friday comes before Easter. The grain of wheat dies and out of it comes new life. Friends, I hope it doesn't sound too melodramatic, but that's the kind of Christian fibre that's going to say to the world: 'We have a unique hope, a great God, a great Saviour, a great Bible and a great hope.'

By faith

So finally, 'through faith'; and that faith you see in these verses. Even if we can't see Jesus, we love him. Even though we don't see the fulfilment, we have inexpressible joy – not just the joy of singing in worship (though I love singing); the inexpressible joy with which they were filled was seen not just in music but in their living day by day. Paul and Silas could sing in prison, not pretending in order to bolster their spirits but out of a real sense that they were in God's will. They rejoiced that they were counted worthy to suffer.

And faith holds on to this great hope. Everything we've talked about this week we hold on to by faith. We believe the Bible is God's word by faith. We believe in that great God – there are many evidences, but belief is still an act of faith. We have every reason to believe; there is no intellectual suicide involved, rather intellectual humility. And we believe that Jesus died and rose again – by faith. And we believe, by faith, that there's an inheritance kept, that our Lord will return, that one day we shall be with him and that one day we shall be like him.

I've almost finished. It seems strange to be studying these first twelve verses of 1 Peter at the end of our conference, because there's a lot more in 1 Peter and I'd love to go on and on and on. But I do want to point out that the very next word in verse 13 is a little three-letter Greek word: *dio*, 'therefore'. And when the argument moves on again in verse 1 of chapter 2 (it's the second word in the Greek), there is another word, *oun*, which is also translated 'therefore'. Peter is saying, 'If this hope is true – what should happen as a result of it?'

Well, read on. Peter says, 'Go and live holy lives. Go and

witness, go and let people know that you have been brought out of darkness into light.' You see, the 'therefore' does not merely imply, 'What a great hope we have, so, therefore, rejoice'; it implies, 'Therefore live holy lives.' And I pray in all humility that because 'We have a hope that is steadfast and certain, Gone through the curtain and touching the throne', we shall have the power to live, as well as to speak, hopefully. For thank God, we have a great hope!

Student celebrations

I

Our relationship with God

by Nigel Lee

Luke 18:9–14; Romans 3:21–26; Psalm 32

It's great to be here. I should think that this is one of the biggest gatherings of students in Britain for many years. I don't know the entirety of what God wants to do in our nation, but I pray that by the time Thursday morning comes God will have set before us, as a group of people involved at the cutting edge of witness in our colleges, a great big vision of himself and his power, of the 'livingness' of his word and what he wants to do among our friends; and that God would so work here that the ripples keep rolling out through our colleges for a long time to come.

Now, let's have a thorough investigation together of the major foundation of our whole spiritual lives. If we're not right on this, then everything else that you hear from tomorrow morning, from 9 o'clock onwards, is likely to rest on a wobbly foundation. You cannot lay the foundation stone yourself. It's something that God has to lay, and it's a strong foundation for everything else that has to follow.

Two men at prayer

Turn with me to Luke's gospel, chapter 18, and read with me verses 9–14.

The Lord Jesus deliberately used that word 'justified' in verse 14. It's a legal term, used when a judge declared somebody not guilty and pronounced that there was no case to be answered against that person any more. It's something that only a judge can pronounce in court. The clerk of the court can't say it; the counsel for the defence can't say it; the accused certainly can't say it. But the judge could say, after all the procedures of the court had been gone through, 'That person is not guilty, and that's an end of the matter. Every single one of those charges that were named in that court cannot ever again be brought against that person.'

And in our whole relationship with God, we must first deal with him as judge. He is a God of law; he is a moral God; he holds us morally responsible. People sometimes try to drive a wedge between Paul and Jesus. They say, 'It's a terrible pity that Paul the apostle used all this legal language when describing our relationship with God and presented him as such an unbending judge. Because really, you know, Jesus only spoke of God as Father. The picture that Jesus gives us is of the father running to welcome and embrace the prodigal as he was coming home all covered in pig muck and rags. That's the picture Jesus gives, but Paul the Pharisee fouled it up.'

But in this passage, it is Jesus who chooses to use that kind of legal language. In fact, look at the previous parable in the first eight verses and you'll see it is all to do with the justice of God's judgment. Jesus is saying that he will be the judge; that we are to face God as our judge. And now the one who is appointed judge, according to those earlier verses, is telling us how this judgment will operate.

Notice, moreover, that one man was able to go home justified from that temple. Here in this life, he was already declared already absolutely in the right with God. Off he goes home as clean as a whistle. In fact, you get the impression from the story that God went home with him and left the other man droning on about his righteousness. It's extraordinary, isn't it? He came to appear before God as we do tonight, and was so conscious of his shortcomings; he went to the temple out of duty, but perhaps he didn't want to get too involved. Maybe he listened to the singing and – perhaps like some of you tonight – his heart was really only half in it. Yes, his mind knew the words, yet his heart wasn't in it and he didn't want to look towards heaven (verse 13).

Has it been a long term? Some of you have had a pretty rough time lately, and you feel you ran out of spiritual resources weeks ago. And you haven't been looking to heaven, not for days, not for weeks; and although you can sing along as well as the person sitting next to you, actually there is something in your heart that hasn't been dealt with. Perhaps you don't even feel worthy to be part of this kind of gathering.

I want you to notice that it is that man and not the other that goes home, who goes back to his chalet, in the right with God.

This is not an isolated thing in the Bible. Scripture everywhere declares it. Abraham in the very first book of the Bible was declared by God to be justified, in the right with God, and he knew it. Paul the apostle preached a bombshell of a sermon in Pisidian Antioch, and in Acts 13:39 he concludes with these words: 'Through him everyone who believes is justified from everything you could not be justified from by the law of Moses.' They must have been gobsmacked – utterly astonished! You see, this is what they would have believed: that you sincerely did your best in your religious and spiritual life, and that when you did wrong, why, you came back and asked for forgiveness. And then you went out and went on your way, and when you did wrong again you could come back and ask for forgiveness and seek God's help a little more next time; and away you went, and you'd come back and you asked for God's forgiveness . . . and so it went on. But the end result of that process would not be published and could not be known until the final great day of judgment. You just couldn't be sure.

It must have been a bombshell, to have listened to Paul telling them that right here, now, today, before they'd even listened to the end of his sermon, they could be absolutely sure long before the end of life that they were going to be declared not guilty, to be told that all charges were settled and dealt with; that God would never turn against them, never turn savage; that they were justified. The man in Jesus' story went home just like that; able to look up to heaven.

And the other man? Well, what a fine religious chap he was! Is there anybody here who fasts twice a week? I bet that in giving a tenth of all he gets he gives a good lot more than some of us. He was a man who was above reproach. He didn't get drunk; there was no hint of sexual immorality or scandal; he was moral, he was upright, he was decent, he was religious.

And maybe he wasn't just the prig that some preachers make him out to be. I guess many of us have heard sermons in which he was portrayed as the most pompous prat you could imagine. And yet I wonder. Did he just go into the quiet of that temple, and there in the shadows begin to go over in his mind how he would stand with God, what his life would have amounted to? And would he begin to say, 'Well, I do this and I do that and I've never fallen into the other'? At the end of his story Jesus says that that man, though he has never slept with his neighbour's wife, though he has never extorted money to which he had no right, though he has always been upright in his religious behaviour – is lost. He's still guilty.

Do you ever think about the day of judgment? Do you imagine the charges being read out? They're all true; and then the Lamb's book of life is called for, and it's brought into the court and the search begins for your name. If the search had begun for this man's name they'd have gone through the book from beginning to end and finally would have had to say, 'The name's not here.' And the man is lost.

Now, how does all this work? If it is legal business, what are the terms? It is quite extraordinary that a man who really has nothing to commend him can be declared righteous for all time with no case to answer, when someone else, who would have made a fine magistrate or church elder – an upright citizen – is condemned.

Read the third chapter of Romans. You see, it's not a matter of God just pretending, and turning a blind eye to the things that are guilty in us and saying that people are quite guilt-free and quite holy and quite acceptable, when in fact they're not. God will not do that. The Bible says very clearly that 'he does not leave the guilty unpunished' (Ex. 34:7).

Some suggest that God's love in the end is so great and so

powerful that it will triumph even over his own holiness. It sounds lofty, doesn't it? What a wonderful thing in God that his love is so great for everybody that it will finally triumph over his own holiness! But that is horrific when you think about it: when the day of judgment comes and everybody is assembled, just as we are assembled here, and God smiles benignly out over the crowd and says to them, 'It's all cancelled. Nothing ever really mattered. Those six million Jews in the Holocaust – not a single one of them mattered. Those people slaughtered in Bosnia – oh, not one of them mattered. The Kurds, slaughtered in their millions; the Somalis, dying because nobody cares – none of them mattered. And two children cut down in Warrington in our own country? Neither of them mattered, either.'

God will not do it.

And you could not go and spend eternity in a heaven with a God who would do it, who would say, 'None of it really mattered, I'm going to cancel the lot and just welcome everybody.' The epistle to the Romans spends the first two and a half chapters proving from every possible conceivable angle that all people everywhere and without exception are unrighteous, are evil. I use the word deliberately.

Now you may say, 'Well, that's a bit strong, that you should call people like that unrighteous and evil.'

I know a great many good, decent, upright people. You would have to use the word 'good' about them. I guess the problem is that we use the word in a variety of different ways. I play the piano a bit. Well, I know two songs. From time to time – it's happened a couple of times in my life – people have come in while I thought I was alone playing my two songs, and they said, 'I didn't know you could play the piano; that's really rather good.' But if Jonathan Lamb, who *can* play the piano, walked into the room you wouldn't ever see me go near a piano. I'd walk out of the room the long way round. I wouldn't admit to playing. But if Mozart came into the room I wouldn't mind betting that even Jonathan would go quiet and leave the piano to Mozart.

You see, we're all good, at our various different levels. The fatal error of the Pharisee in the story was to mistake the level that God was on, the level relevant to him. He thought that all that was necessary was to secure a higher score than the tax collector, but you and I face judgment according to an absolute sense of goodness. And God has been kind enough in that story, and in the passage we're about to read, to show us what the verdict in our life can absolutely, for sure, be.

Justified freely by his grace

Let's read then Romans 3:21–26. God has unveiled something quite new (verse 21). He'd been dropping hints about it for centuries through the prophets, and sometimes the hints got so close. Read Isaiah 53 – it's astonishing. All through the Old Testament the prophets had been dropping their hints, but now, says Paul, it's here; a different kind of righteousness altogether, quite unlike that which people are brainwashed to seek when they begin to think about God.

It has three features, says Paul. One, it is nothing to do with the law (verse 21). It is a righteousness that is not achieved by reaching a pass mark or by having to qualify. Secondly (verse 22), it comes direct from God, for believers in Jesus. It's like a bank transfer. Into your overdraft account comes an enormous amount of credit at the push of a button. There it goes! And it is free to you. It is a gift. The word he uses (verse 24) is 'redemption'.

In the first century it was possible to get into such terrible debt that there would come a time when you had nothing left with which to pay. Everything you had, had been repossessed. The only thing you had left was yourself, and now that had to be sold into slavery to pay your debt. And a relative or perhaps even somebody who cared for you very much might at that point step in and buy you back out of slavery, paying what you could not pay, so that you could remain free.

'That is what God has done,' says Paul. 'It's got nothing to do with people keeping the law; you're already beyond hope of rescue by the law. This is something that those who believe in Jesus find happens to them. It is a free gift, a buying out of slavery for those who don't deserve it, and it's once and for all.'

Understand this. God doesn't look at your life in little

moral segments, so that when something goes wrong you get forgiven for that segment, then you try hard for a few days and then another segment goes wrong and so you get forgiven for that bit. 'No!' the Bible says in Hebrews 9:27: it's given unto people once to die, and only then comes the judgment, and it is a judgment on your entire life, the whole lot taken together: and if there is one sin found in that whole life, you are a sinner. How many sins did it take Adam to become a sinner? You won't be any different.

This passage is about God's fairness. Our whole lives are looked at together, and that is why Paul can go on to say, 'All have sinned and fall short' (verse 23). And God did not give up his Son for isolated little bits of your life but wholly, for your entire life. You faced one judgment, and you received one salvation in Christ that covers everything. You are declared justified and you can know it now.

I've heard people say, 'But that's not fair. It's not right that an innocent third party should suffer for someone else's sin. That's unjust.' And what they say is absolutely true. It *wouldn't* be right or fair for a third party to suffer in a case like this. But this is the wonder of it; this is at the heart of New Testament Christianity. *There is no third party*. It is God himself who loved us and gave up his Son, the second person of the Trinity.

God is a team. God acts with one heart and one mind. There is one God, and he gave up his Son with whom he was one, as a sacrifice of atonement. He was the one wronged and he has taken the initiative to put it right, and he's done it like this in order to demonstrate just how fair and just God really is. Look at verses 25–26: 'He did this to demonstrate his justice' – justice to those who committed sin before the cross.

He is absolutely fair to those who died before Jesus came, manifest in flesh. We have no more or no less law to keep than those in the Old Testament. Salvation was by faith for Abraham; it was so for Moses; it was so for David; it was so for Isaiah; it was so for the thief on the cross, and it is so for us. God is fair to the people who have never heard of the Old Testament law. They are saved by faith as they come and say, 'O God, I need mercy, I need help.' He is absolutely fair to the type of person who finds that religion comes more easily to them. There are some people who find religion easy, and there are some who find it very, very difficult. God is fair to both. It has nothing to do with what some people find easy. It is salvation by faith, by grace; you ask, you receive, it's a free bank draft, it is a redemption, it comes from God.

And God will remain fair and just all the way through eternity. He won't suddenly charge you with things for which Christ has died. God will not hold sin against you. I don't believe the Bible teaches that God will actually forget sin; but he will not hold it against you. He doesn't erase all the stuff of this life from his knowledge.

Imagine meeting Jesus in heaven. You're walking down a golden street, and there is Jesus strolling along towards you. He catches sight of you. 'Oh, nice to see you. You did make it; that's wonderful!'

And you say, 'Excuse me, Jesus, I've just noticed. Those holes in your hands – what are they doing there?'

'Holes?' says Jesus, 'Holes? Dear me – I don't know. I haven't the slightest idea how they got there. I never noticed them before.'

Do you think that is likely? *He knows why they're there*. And so will you. The very subject of the praise of heaven is the Lamb who was slain. There will be an amazing awareness of just how much he has done for us. We will know that we were sinners and we will know that we're absolutely safe. He will not ever charge us with those things. He will not hold them against us.

Justified: declared not guilty, not any more, not ever. Does this mean that all sinners everywhere are therefore somehow right with God, because Christ died for the whole world? That everybody is somehow made ready for heaven like a kind of oven-ready chicken, all just proceeding happily towards heaven?

Certainly not. Verse 26 says that a response on our part is demanded: '. . . and the one who justifies those who have faith in Jesus'. He justifies those who do not trust themselves, who don't appear before God to put on a big show and make a religious speech as that Pharisee prayed about himself. They trust not themselves, but his gift. They obey not their own whims and desires, but him. Being right with God starts with an attitude of your own heart, as you turn and simply say, 'Lord, thank you. Please include me in.'

And if your heart, even though you come here, is still turned away; if you're still insisting on your own goodness, your own will and your own little stubbornness as you barge your way through life; then, says the Bible, you are not yet right with God.

A psalm of justification

Turn with me finally to Psalm 32:1. 'Blessed is he whose transgressions are forgiven' – their whole burden is taken away; 'whose sins are covered' – are concealed, put out of sight. There are two reasons for happiness. And then he repeats it in the next verse. 'Blessed is the man whose sin the LORD does not count against him' – and then he goes on: in whose spirit there has come to be a change, there's no longer deceit. God is working in that person's heart. His sin is forgiven; he's met the judge; he's been declared not guilty; and God has begun to change his spirit. Happy that man!

Then David gives something of his own testimony. 'When I kept silent, my bones wasted away through my groaning all day long. For day and night your hand was heavy upon me; my strength was sapped as in the heat of summer.' What a time of agony! Do any of you identify with this? You've felt guilty, you've felt rotten; you know that you're not right with God, that things have gone wrong, and that you feel physically weak. You lack energy. There's an inward tension and a groaning. The nights are horrible because you feel restless and the dawn brings no relief. 'Day and night your hand was heavy upon me.'

And then in the next verse the boil seems to burst, and it all comes out. 'Then I acknowledged my sin to you and did not cover up my iniquity.' I said: Lord, enough of that. It's ruining my life. 'And you forgave the guilt of my sin.' David knew it to be true in his own experience. God forgave.

So what happens? He can rejoice. The last verse says: 'Rejoice in the LORD and be glad, you righteous; sing, all you who are upright in heart!' (verse 11). This is the foundation of real lasting joy. I do sometimes meet in my travels students who seem to me to be extraordinarily weighed down and miserable. You need a kind of theological joy in your life, all the time. There's a theological foundation to joy in life – we've seen it at this conference already; and it's also the basis of your relationships with other people: that God has accepted you and that God has accepted those people you perhaps find it difficult, sometimes, to live with.

We haven't had our first night here yet. So we haven't had the snoring. It'll be interesting in the morning! You know, it's really difficult to accept someone lovingly in Christ at 3 o'clock in the morning when you haven't slept a wink, or when the guy's socks are walking round at night, you know, a sort of night light squeaking and glowing in the dark, because he hasn't been home yet and he only took two socks to the beginning of term.

The people who worship God differently think differently about many issues. But the fundamental question – whether they snore or not, whatever their socks are like, or whether they are just theologically different – is, is this person in Christ? Because if God has accepted him or her in the same way that the thief was accepted and that tax collector was accepted, then what are you doing turning your nose up at this brother or sister? You have no right. We accept each other because of justification. We feel secure in God because of what God has done and promised. And we can cope with the things that happen to us. You might fail your examinations. Well, I think when I've done my stint at UCCF I'll start up a new movement for those people who've failed; because God accepts us just as we are.

Finally, it gives us the message that we can go out and proclaim. You know, people commit suicide in the places where we live and work, because they just don't know God and they feel nobody cares for them. There are people who've gone home in the last few days, but they've hardly got a home to go to because their parents have split up while they've been away. There are people who are wracked with guilt. They don't know God. They don't know what God thinks of them. They don't know whether God understands what it's like to be them. They've got their tutors and teachers snarling at them and they feel an utter failure. Some of them are in a vice-like grip to certain habits. Some of them carry around with them appalling guilt. Are they friends of yours?

You are able to tell them of a God who will accept people like the ones we've seen this evening. He will accept them for ever. He wants to be their friend, he wants to begin to change them. He will set all their guilt and their rottenness upon his Son and it will be gone for ever, and that Son who loved them so much will then come and walk with them every day through life. What a tremendous thing to be able to tell people!

We could transform people, colleges and universities, if this message, this simple stuff, could get into the hearts and the minds of people whom we know. It's no wonder that David says, 'Then I will teach transgressors your ways' (Ps. 51:13) – I'm going to talk about you, God. Because God says you can be free. You can be forgiven. You can know it. You can be sure you are accepted just as you are. Isn't it exciting? Isn't it thrilling? What are you going to do with that? Are you going to go and take it and tell someone? Go on! Amen!

2

God sends his rescuer

by Hugh Palmer

Colossians 1:15–23

To be alienated from God is to have no communication with our heavenly Father. But the apostle says, it's more than that: it's not just that we are alienated, but that in truth we are enemies in our minds.

I imagine we don't like that kind of talk. It's not the way we speak. We speak of people being close to God; the apostle says they're estranged. We speak of people being sympathetic, or perhaps at worst apathetic; he says they're enemies. We really don't know our own hearts and minds very well.

There's a poignant story of an American gangster called Two-Gun Crowley, who was finally arrested after 150 police had cornered him in his flat and pumped several rounds of bullets and tear-gas pellets into the place. While he was under siege there, he managed to write a note which was found on him when they captured him. 'Under my coat', he had written, 'is a weary heart but a kind one, one that would do nobody any harm.' After he was arrested he was tried and sentenced to the electric chair for shooting a policeman who'd asked him for his driving licence. 'A weary heart but a kind one, one that would do nobody any harm' – but would shoot a policeman if he asked for his driving licence.

We pass very kind verdicts on ourselves. Probably few of us would declare ourselves enemies of God, and few of our friends would do so either. But what else is to be made of our defiance of God? Whether he woos us as a lover or commands us as Lord, people go on turning their backs on him and resisting his orders. I was missioning up in Norfolk the other week and I found it almost every night: the very polite, British, way of being an enemy of God.

It went like this. As I stood by the door at the end of the

evening, whether we had been in a pub or a formal dinner or somebody's home, and as I said goodbye, people would look at me as they went out and say, 'Thank you for a lovely evening.' That was their way of declaring they were enemies with God.

I'm not just guessing, for I asked some of them, 'I'm glad you enjoyed it. Tell me, what did you make of Jesus?' (I'd explained the claims of Jesus as clearly as I could.)

'Fascinating, but not for me,' said one.

'Well, you see now, I thought it was interesting but I don't think it does anything for me,' said another.

'No, I don't think so. I've got Buddhist beliefs,' said a third (much to the surprise of her husband!).

The language couldn't be more polite, could it? But what else are we really to make of this civilized veneer that hides a determined defiance of God? What else are we to conclude of the treatment of God's people?

Do you remember when the apostle Paul was converted on the Damascus road and that voice from heaven cried out to him, 'Saul, Saul, why are you persecuting me?' As far as we know he'd never raised a finger against Jesus. But we are told that he set out for Damascus breathing murderous threats against the Lord's disciples.

Well, our world hasn't changed. The history of the twentieth century reeks with stories of violence and oppression to the Christian church. You can tour almost the entire globe and find it – the Soviet Union, China, Cambodia, Africa, Nepal . . . . Statisticians tell us that there have been more martyrs in this century than in the whole of the rest of history. Our society acts the same way. The media love to climb aboard the latest controversy that'll do down the Christian church. How many times have Students Unions barred Christian Unions from holding meetings on their premises? How many sneers, taunts and snide comments, and just joining in the helpless mockery, goes on towards the individual Christian?

What is God to make of those? Aren't they the mouths of an enemy? Isn't this description of us all too true? 'Alienated from God . . . enemies in [our] minds' (verse 21).

Now the problem of sin goes deeper than me and the mess I make of my life, deeper than society and the mess we're making of this world. We have offended God. We have declared ourselves to be his enemies, we have put ourselves in line for his just judgments. You will remember that last night Nigel pointed out to us that we are all of us in this state. All have sinned, and it matters. And when we take on board the awfulness of sin, when it comes to talking about different religions, the question we have to ask about a religion is not 'Does it do me good?' but 'Does it save me?' The Saviour I need to look for is not a Saviour who counts with me, but a Saviour who counts with God. The awfulness of sin is that it leaves me alienated from God, an enemy in my mind.

The wonder of reconciliation

But of course the Christian message doesn't stop there. As our eyes open to the awfulness of sin, so you find the gospel wants to tell us about the wonder of reconciliation. Gerald Priestland, who was the BBC's Religious Affairs Correspondent, once said that when he was ten years old he realized that Christianity spoke a lot about sin. By the time he was fifteen he had glimpses into the abyss of depression, accompanied by fears of divine vengeance for his unnameable secret crimes. I dread to think what he had done by that age that deserved that description; but those fears, he said, kept growing for the next thirty years. And Christianity was no help to him. He said, 'I looked at the cross and I saw the suffering Christ, and its only message was – "You did this and there is no health in you."'

There is something very tragic, is there not, about someone who's understood verse 21 and never read as far as verse 22. There's something tragic when the Christian message is twisted to be all about sin instead of the forgiving of sin. 'Once you were alienated from God and were enemies in your minds because of your evil behaviour. But now he has reconciled you by Christ's physical body through death to present you holy in his sight, without blemish and free from accusation.' That's the wonder of reconciliation. If only someone had told Gerald Priestland about verse 22!

Now as Paul describes Jesus, God's Christ, in the verses that we have in front of us, he is describing the rescuer king whom God provides. Look back to verse 19: 'For God was pleased to have all his fulness dwell in him' – but notice that verse 20 is also part of what God was pleased to do: 'and through him to reconcile to himself all things.' God was pleased: here's the Saviour with whom he was pleased.

Look at verse 22: God has done the reconciling. Here's the salvation that counts with the person with whom it really needs to count: God himself. That's the wonder of it. And look at what it's accomplished: we can be 'presented' – that's actually a legal word, used when somebody is taken to court and presented there; we can be presented before the divine judge. The reconciled Christian is found faultless, 'holy in his sight, without blemish and free from accusation'.

'Holy' means someone set apart for God, as does the word 'saint'. I remember once, in one of those awkward discussions that tend to follow when people discover you're a clergyman, finding myself in a protracted conversation on this very subject. I took a deep breath and said, 'The whole idea of canonizing anyone undermines the entire Christian gospel.' It fuelled the discussion even more; but I wanted to say it, because when the New Testament calls someone a saint, it doesn't demand that they should have an exemplary life to their credit, it doesn't demand that they should have worked any miracles; all it looks for is the work that Jesus accomplished on the cross. And that's what's being said here.

'Without blemish, free from accusation.' They used to say that Ronald Reagan benefited from the 'Teflon factor' – because no mud stuck to him! Well, Christians are Teflon men and women. We're free from accusation. None of it will stick. That's the wonder of reconciliation.

The uniqueness of the rescuer

Someone who has taken in much of what we've being saying so far may well say, 'That's great, I'm so pleased for you.' But if that is what you are saying, you've still missed the point. It's not a matter of having pleased someone else. This is the rescue, God's reconciliation, and when we read from verse 15 onwards, we can't help but be struck by *the uniqueness of the rescuer*.

One of the most pervasive and the most deceitful of today's philosophies is relativism. We live in an age in which people like to think there are no absolutes. Of course it's a flawed philosophy, with a massive contradiction right at its heart: the implied contradiction, 'There are no absolutes except this statement that there no absolutes'! Logically, a relativist viewpoint ought to prevent anyone from talking about the truth, or categorizing something as wrong. But the biblical framework uses both those concepts. Jesus said, 'I am the truth,' and he turned on some of his religious opponents and said, 'You are wrong.' But relativism is one of the most undermining forces against the gospel – and it's everywhere. It's permeated our society; it's certainly permeated the campus, the church and the Christian Unions.

And when it comes to the issue of the uniqueness of God's rescuer king, God's Christ, I think that relativism assumes two forms. The crude version says, 'All religions are the same.' It's like saying that all Chinese look alike. It tells you far more about the observer's ignorance than it does about either religions or the Chinese. To say that all religions are the same is nonsense. They differ in their view of God, of how many gods there are, and whether there is a God at all. Yet we throw this view out as a lifeline to the Buddhist, Hindu or Muslim whom we fear might be offended by exclusive claims made for Christ.

The error of relativism

Well – those exclusive claims may indeed cause offence; but so will that line of argument; for they don't think their religion is the same either. So a more sophisticated version is often argued that goes something like this: 'Well, it's all a matter of personal preference. Great, I'm so pleased for you – but it's not for me.' This view holds that all religions are just different paths to the top of the same mountain. One Indian writer put it this way: that as one can ascend to the top of a house by means of a ladder or a bamboo or a staircase or a rope, so diverse are the ways and means to approach God, and every religion in the world shows one of those ways.

There is something very attractive in such talk. Many of us have no doubt subscribed to it at one time or another – or perhaps still do. For we're likely to do so if we want to shrink from the seeming arrogance of exclusive claims about Jesus. We do so if we are anxious to appear tolerant in a pluralistic society, when we understand we are mixing with people of other faiths and we want to respect them.

The tragedy, of course, is that we are left with precisely the arrogance that the relativist struggles to avoid. For when you tell me that all religions are the same or they all lead to the top of the same mountain, you're not just saying the Christians are wrong, you're saying the Muslims are wrong too; for they don't think their religion is taking them to the same place as ours is. I don't believe for a moment that down the road in the local mosque they believe that what they're teaching will take their followers to the same place as the gospel of Jesus Christ.

You will have noticed by now that the problem with the relativist's position is that the only person who's got it right is not the Christian, or the Muslim, or the Hindu, or the Buddhist, or the Taoist – but the relativist; the only person who's actually spotted what's really going on. You can't get much more arrogant than that! And the other problem is that relativism avoids pluralism rather than faces it. It can come to terms with the difference in religions only by saying they're not really different at all – as if there were many ways to God.

To hold to that position, we would actually have to do a lot of rewriting of the passage that we've been looking at. And I want now to point out just some of the things we would have to deny.

First, if there are many ways to God, we need to deny the supremacy of Christ. Look at the paragraph beginning at verse 15. It's a remarkable paragraph and we haven't got time to look at it properly tonight. But if you ever think your Jesus is too small, go and read this paragraph again. I can't put some other figure alongside Jesus without denying verses 15–20, can I? Look at those phrases – 'by him', he is 'before all things', they're all 'created by him', in him they all 'hold together', he sustains all things. And they were created not only by him but for him. All our futures lead to him. We will not all one day come face to face with the Buddha, we will not all one day come face to face with Muhammad – we will all one day come face to face with Jesus Christ.

Do you see the emphasis in verse 19? Not just 'his fulness' but 'all his fulness'. It's very precise. I can't squeeze anyone between God and this Christ.

Now, it's no good saying, 'We can't speak like this today, we're in a pluralist society.' So were they! This was a message written to a group of young Christians in a tiny minority in a town where there were many other religions around. The apostle is writing to tell them that the good news they have heard about this Christ is sufficient to take them to the God who made them and for whom they were destined. He was writing to tell them that they could close their ears to the other siren voices in their city: the Judaizers, the astrologers, the super-spiritual ones, the first-century equivalent of New Age channelling, all of which begin to be explained in the next chapter.

And then verse 20 – I know we've looked at it before, but look at the scope of it: 'all things, whether things on earth or things in heaven, by making peace through his blood, shed on the cross'. All things – it's very exclusive, isn't it? It may prove too much for some people's liking. But it doesn't leave room for any other saviour. This one has reconciled all things. Of course in another sense it's very *inclusive*. As an ex-Hindu friend of mine loves to put it: Jesus died for Hindus, died for Muslims, died for Sikhs, died for New Agers.

Next, how am I saved? How do I get to God's kingdom? Oh, the options are multitudinous today – the five pillars of

Islam, the law of Moses, the sevenfold path of enlighten-
ment, sacrifices, alms-giving – they're all claimed as ways to
lead you to ultimate bliss. But Jesus is very different. 'I am
the way,' he says. 'No-one comes to the Father except
through me' (Jn. 14:6). And this just says the same thing in
another way – God was pleased through Jesus to reconcile
to himself all things. I cannot call another person 'saviour' or
another path 'salvation' without denying this truth about
Christ. That is why C. S. Lewis said that Christianity is
either the greatest truth or a monstrous hoax. The one thing
it cannot be is merely of moderate importance.

Christ is a unique rescuer. To say there are many ways to
God is to deny the truth about Christ; it's to deny the
necessity of the cross. The attraction of relativism is that it
frees us from so many hard questions about God and from
the apparent sense of unfairness if we've got to back only
Jesus. That seems to remove a level playing field; but the
problem with poor apologetic and poor reasoning is that it
only backs us into an impossible corner somewhere else.
Look how verse 20 ends: God was pleased through Christ to
reconcile to himself all things, 'by making peace through his
blood, shed on the cross'. Nigel was talking about this to us
last night.

We may find it hard to believe that it took the cross to
rescue us. We may find it hard to believe that we're in such a
mess that God had to give his one and only Son to die such a
death to save us. But we must find it *impossible* to believe,
must we not, that if he did there would be an alternative
rescue. That would be monstrous of God, if there were.
Imagine the scene: Jesus returns to heaven, scars and all.
And he's hardly settled down and made himself at home
again, when the executive calls another meeting, the outreach secretary does his job and brings salvation on to the
agenda; and they ask, 'Well, Jesus, that's good, we've got
this rescue in place. Now, how else shall we let people in?'

That's ludicrous. I'm a parent; I've only got one son.
Don't ask me to defend the love of a God who gave his Son
to die such a death, who abandoned him and forsook him –
if it were not necessary. 'There must be more than one way

to God' – how dare we say that? It makes a mockery of the cross. It denies the truth about the rescuer. It denies the necessity of the cross.

It denies, lastly, the universality of the gospel. It denies, in fact, that the gospel is a gospel for the whole world; for that is precisely what is said in the last verse in this paragraph. Look at that last sentence in verse 23: 'This is the gospel that you heard and that has been proclaimed to every creature under heaven, and of which I, Paul, have become a servant.' God has in principle reconciled to himself the whole of creation, from the aardvark to the zebra if you like. God in Christ proclaimed that once-for-all reconciliation, his heralds are scurrying to the four ends of the earth with the news, and, says Paul, he's one of them. 'I am a servant of that gospel.'

It's not an apostolic claim. It's not just apostles who are servants of the gospel. He calls at least two other people in this letter fellow-servants with him. He's just explaining why he's writing to people he has never met: because he's a servant of a gospel, a gospel which is for people wherever they are on the earth.

Now to be a servant of the gospel is just another way of describing a Christian. Paul says that this gospel that focused around Jesus, God's Christ, God's rescuer king, is a gospel 'that you heard'; it happened and it has been 'proclaimed to every creature under heaven'. Now that wasn't true, was it? Every creature under heaven had not heard the gospel. Ah, but they would; it's got to go to all the ends of the world; there's something about the gospel that guarantees it. When it truly gets into us, we've got to get it out of us; it's that kind of gospel. That's why the New Testament writes in this way.

If I visit a Christian Union and I find it has no missionary concern, am I not entitled to ask if it's really got a gospel? It doesn't appear to have *this* gospel. If I find a Christian who's not telling his or her friends or not wanting to bring them under the sound of the gospel, am I not entitled to ask if the gospel is truly in them? For where is the sign of this 'must get to the ends of the earth' gospel? 'There are many ways to

God,' someone says; am I not entitled to ask if the gospel is really in them? How do they square their ideas with the idea that we must get this gospel to every creature under heaven?

More of that tomorrow night. But as we finish, I would like to make this ideal of a universal gospel, a gospel for everyone, more personal.

Ameena is in her early twenties; she's from a Sikh family but she's been a Christian for about two and a half years now. As is often the case when people convert to Christ from a different religion and a different culture, the real friction (disturbing though the moment of conversion is) begins when someone is baptized. Towards the end of last year, Ameena was due to be baptized. When the day came and it was time for the service to start, there was no sign of her. Then the telephone rang: the terse voice of a relative announced that Ameena wasn't coming. Obviously she was being kept at home.

But twenty minutes later Ameena turned up. The service went ahead. The minister was standing in the baptismal pool with Ameena and was preparing to ask her some questions about her faith when there was a disturbance at the back. Two men made their way politely but firmly through the congregation to the front.

Ameena's elder brother spoke on behalf of the family. He was not aggressive, but he was very firm and his words were clear. He confronted that small group of Christians: 'Ameena is of an age where she can speak for herself, and can make up her own mind. We know that and we respect it. But we want you to know, and we want her to know, that if she goes through with this baptism this morning, the family home is closed to her.'

When they'd said what they had come to say they made their way out. The minister, who was still in the pool, simply turned to Ameena and put to her the questions he was going to ask her anyway.

'Ameena, do you repent of your sins?'

'I repent of my sins.'

'Ameena, do you turn to Christ?'

'I turn to Christ.'

When we say there must be many ways to God, doesn't it occur to us that we're really saying, 'Ameena, you needn't have bothered?' People who have converted to Christ from other faiths have died for doing it. When we're saying there must be many ways to God we're saying they needn't have bothered, that this gospel isn't the gospel that has to be the gospel for everyone.

If I deny the truth about Christ and supremacy of Christ, if I deny the necessity of the cross, if I deny the universality of the gospel, if I deny the rescuer whom God has provided – if I deny all that and still want to talk about God, it must be a different God I am talking about.

Bob Hope, in one of his little flippant one-liners, once said this: 'I do benefits for all religions; I'd hate to blow the hereafter on a technicality.'

He won't. No-one will blow the hereafter on a technicality. We can only blow it on an essential: Jesus.

3

God's heart for the world

by Dick Dowsett

Acts 17:1–34

This passage is the word of God and you can trust it completely, which isn't remotely true of my preaching! So please will you keep your Bible open, because if you see it in the Scriptures then you are to do as you're told, and if you don't see it in the Scriptures it's just Dick Dowsett rubbish and you can throw it out.

It is amazing being in a lovely big gathering like this, isn't it? I wonder how many times over we could fill this hall with Christian young people from Britain. It's a particularly fascinating thought for me as I think about Turkey with a population about the same as Britain, and considerably fewer believers in the whole country than there are in this hall tonight. Or when I think about the Sudanese for whom I'm burdened, or the island of Java in Indonesia – about half the population of Britain, and probably not as many believers as there are in one block of you sitting here. Or as I think of a Korean colleague of mine, who found in Seoul that he could evangelize and plant a church in a year; and in four years in Japan, with all those gifts and experience, he has been able to lead two Japanese to Christ. As a Japanese said to me in a coffee bar, 'We Japanese don't want to become Christians.' And can you even begin to go up that high mountain with the Lord Jesus, where the devil showed him all the nations of the earth and said, 'They are mine'?

Do you sometimes feel that Jesus is a sort of also-ran, that you're not quite sure whether he's really worth betting on? And then you come back to that great commission which Jesus gives, where he says, 'I call the shots in heaven and I call the shots on earth – so as you go about, make people let me call the shots in their lives.' Or, if you want it more traditionally, 'All authority in heaven and on earth has been given to me. Therefore go and make disciples of all nations, . . . teaching them to obey everything I have commanded you' (Mt. 28:18-20); not to pick and choose, but to submit and to bow the knee.

Do you find that when you think of countries like most of the Islamic world, with its nine hundred million, very few of whom have ever thought of becoming Christians – do you find yourself *really* believing that there is salvation in no-one else, because there is no other name given under the sky whereby people can be saved (as Peter, when he was truly Spirit-filled, proclaimed in Acts 4:12)? You see, in a way we know it. We know that there's no-one like Jesus, we know that there is no other Saviour. And yet so often our reaction to that is to have stimulating discussion groups about whether or not the unevangelized can possibly find a back door, or debating whether it's possible that a Muslim might be saved by Jesus even though he has never trusted him.

But these convictions of the Scripture are not meant to lead us into discussion groups. They are meant to mobilize us for a lost world. And this is what we see that they did for the apostle Paul in this chapter we have before us. And I want us to look at it in two halves.

Paul in Thessalonica

The first half is where he's evangelizing in the synagogue, because in that half we find the apostle Paul doing something very significant. He is beginning his missionary burden with outreach to people who are culturally just the same as him; and that is where most of us are going to begin. It's utter hog-wash for us to be challenged at Word Alive by the world, if we believe that one day we're going to get on a jumbo jet and fly off somewhere and start evangelizing even though we've never done it before. There is something very sick about running away to evangelize Mexico or Eastern Europe if you've never actually talked to your own classmates about Jesus.

The strategy

So Paul began with his own people. He went to the Jews first; he had a natural bridge, they were his own people, a people who were prepared to look at the Scriptures. God had intended them to be a light to the ethnic groups – the Gentiles, as our Bible traditionally translates it. I want to suggest to you that Paul gives us a model here; a model of going first where he was culturally at home.

Now think about this: what sort of ministry was it that he had there in Thessalonica? He says that it was a ministry from the Scriptures, verse 2. In verse 11 he got the people to examine the Scriptures; in verse 13 he says he preached the word of God. True, he was in an environment where people would take the Scriptures seriously, but they weren't all Jews who were there.

I want to say to you that one of the things that has thrilled me doing university missions in different parts of the world is the way that unbelievers are gobsmacked when they look at the Scriptures. A few years ago we saw it in Glasgow University. Many of the students said to me, 'If you put out John's gospels they'll just throw them away,' but they couldn't believe it when they saw their non-Christian friends working at the Scriptures, writing their notes and comments on the gospels. We saw the same last year in Szeged and Pecs in Hungary, where most of the folk there had never before read anything out of the Bible; analysing, looking at what the Scriptures have to say about the Lord Jesus Christ. But the evangelism that Paul did was not bashing people with the Bible, still less bashing them with five standard texts. Because, you see, he took unbelievers into an in-depth examination of Scripture.

Do you see the sort of words that are used here? Verse 3, he 'proclaimed' the gospel. In other words, we're not going to have a discussion on the basis of ignorance. You have got to tell them something about what the gospel is. But he didn't just proclaim the gospel, for it says in verse 2, 'he reasoned with them'. He was prepared to dialogue, to reason with them, to explain it and to apply it to their lives..

He does not, as it were, put their opinions on the back-burner, and say, 'Shut up, I must get to page 4 before you talk.' He 'explained' the Scriptures to them, it says in verse 3, and that is tremendously important. So many are like that mature student from Ethiopia whom Philip encountered in his Daimler – that Ethiopian Chancellor of the Exchequer who made that endearing comment, 'Yes, it's great to have a bit of the Bible. But how on earth can I understand it unless somebody explains it to me?'

But in verse 3 it also says that he 'proved' things. He didn't say, 'Just take it or leave it;' he said, 'Come on – let's give you some evidence.' He didn't say to them, 'You've just got to swallow hard and believe it, even though it sounds absolute nonsense.' He says, 'Let me give you some reasons why you can take this seriously.' So in verse 11, in Berea, the people were able to check it out for themselves and see that it was so. You see, evangelism wasn't just bashing people with four or five texts. That's how I began to evangelize; with four texts from Romans that said nothing about Jesus except one five-letter word in one of the texts. Everybody got processed starting with Romans 3:23 and ending up with Romans 10:9. If I didn't start at Romans 3:23, I couldn't get to 10:9, for I didn't know how to do it any other way.

That's all right, I had to begin somewhere. But that's kindergarten evangelism. It's not what Paul's doing here. Paul is getting them to think and to interact, and the result is that serious seekers get saved.

Unfortunately the NIV doesn't believe in the divine inspiration of conjunctions. There's one that is in the Greek, which they leave out in verses 11–12. It says that with great eagerness they 'examined the Scriptures every day to see if what Paul said was true'; therefore 'Many of the Jews believed'. Serious seekers, who were encouraged to suss it out for themselves, got saved. In Thessalonica they were, as verse 4 puts it, 'persuaded'. That's very important, isn't it?

I was up in Stirling once. A bright spark there was keenly evangelizing an Egyptian Muslim. He said, 'Never mind about your problems and your questions; just open your heart to Jesus.'

But the Muslim said to me, 'Well, I opened my heart to Jesus and nothing happened.'

So I said to him, he being a Muslim, 'Aren't you thrilled to bits with the way the Lord Jesus died on the cross for you?'

He replied, 'He never did! God would never allow his holy prophet to die on a cross.'

And I thought – 'Hello, who's this idiot who is asking this man to open his heart to Jesus when he doesn't even believe that he died on the cross?'

What sort of Jesus is left, if you say, 'I don't want the one that died on the cross'? There isn't any other. So now do you see the importance of it? We've got to take the word of God seriously, we've got to take seriously the minds, the problems and the questions of the people to whom we are talking. Above all that, brothers and sisters, the thing that you find so brilliant about the apostle Paul is that *he talks about Jesus*.

Have you noticed that? He didn't find it very easy. He said to the Ephesians, 'You've got to pray for me that I actually declare the gospel as I ought to' (*cf.* Eph. 6:19–20). He was a chicken like the rest of us, but he knew that the thing that was really going to get people turned on was to talk about Jesus. And he talks about Jesus – look at those early verses – Jesus who had to die, who is risen, who is the only one who could save people. He approached this in all sorts of different ways. He was a bit different in Athens from how he was in Thessalonica, but the big question is: are you actually prepared to talk about Jesus?

When I was an undergraduate I went back to my home church and I said to the minister, 'What can I do to help?'

He said, 'Get in among them and talk about Jesus. They'll talk about anything except him.' It's true and it's tragic.

The result

But what was the result of Paul's mission, in his own cultural environment, there in the synagogue?

The first thing is that *people were converted*. Who? Well, he says, there were many people who were just like him and there were others who weren't a bit like him, who were ethnically different from him. And the thing that we need to understand here is that in our own culture you can do cross-cultural mission with people who actually already speak brilliant English. That's wonderful, because language study is an absolute pain in the neck, I can tell you. (On one occasion in the Philippines, I told the congregation, 'You must give birth again, it's the only way you are going to get saved.') But, you see, there were people there in the synagogue who could already read the Jewish scriptures, but they were ethnically different.

Don't you realize the amazing opportunities that are here? I have a burden for the Uygur people in North-West China. I never expected to meet Uygur people in Glasgow – would you? But I did. I have a burden for Mongolians. I never expected to meet Mongolians among students in Budapest – would you? But I did. Wherever you go there is an amazing opportunity for us in our own culture: yes, to meet and reach our own folk – but there are others who are easier than they would be otherwise, and they were there in Paul's cultural environment. Don't postpone mission, thinking, 'One of these days I'm going to get involved in world mission' – it's here in your own culture.

But I want you to understand that *people made trouble* when they really started getting involved in these ways. In verse 6 people said that this sort of missionary work was socially disruptive. 'These people are turning the world upside down' – that wasn't a compliment, it was an insult. 'Whenever these Christians come, everything gets inside out and back to front and it's a right old mess.'

Of course it was a lie, but people say it's very socially disruptive to have real evangelism going on. They said that it was politically explosive (verse 7). And as Paul got involved with evangelism even in his own culture, he became frightened. He wrote to the Thessalonians: 'We had a terrible time in Philippi, but we had courage in our God to declare the gospel of God in the face of great opposition' (*cf.* 1 Thes. 2:2). It took guts – and God had to give us guts.

Are you frightened? Is that the reason that probably only a handful in each Christian Union are really actively trying to reach unbelievers – because they are scared? God knows it's frightening. But we need to do it.

Paul in Athens

But the opportunity came for Paul to reach out beyond his own people-group, and he went over to Athens.

The other week I was speaking at a conference for the KGK (the Japanese UCCF), and I went one day to the city of Aurora which is on the outskirts of Tokyo. My host, who was a Korean, gave me a leaflet in English that contained a map of the city with all the significant places highlighted. Fifty per cent of them were temples. The rest were the hospital, Post Office and so on. I wondered, 'Where are the churches?' I looked right through the tourist information. There were no churches, only temples to this and temples to that. I thought, 'This is just like Athens!' Then they told me of the goals they had for their city. They were so Stoic it wasn't true; and I thought, 'This is amazing! It's Athens all over again.'

Athens was the cultural centre of the Graeco-Roman world. It was a great university town, now a bit past its best. And it was full of idols; it really was the most amazing, pluralistic society, like Thailand with its ubiquitous spirit houses, or Japan with more Buddhas than people. It was 'very religious' (verse 22). The world is very religious; and certainly, among the great religions of the world we have not begun to make an impact. There are so few Hindus, Muslims and Buddhists who have come to Christ, but the world is 'very religious'. In 1986 there were somewhere between 300 and 400 new religions registered in Japan – 'very religious'. And full of the latest ideas; that's Athens as well (verse 21); they are always wanting to talk. They, with T. S. Eliot's Prufrock, had this motto: 'I have measured out my life with coffee spoons.'[1]

They were open to new ideas, but were very un-committed. A survey determined that 75% of Japanese

1. T. S. Eliot, 'The Love Song of J. Alfred Prufrock', in *Collected Poems 1909–1935* (Faber & Faber, 1936).

young people, if they had to choose a religion, would choose Christianity. The trouble is, they don't have to choose a religion – or they think they don't. Interested, uncommitted: cities are great places of opportunity if you have a heart like Paul's. What sort of heart? A heart that was prepared to be moved by ungodliness. Is yours?

A friend of mine in Japan said, 'If another British tourist comes and says, "Oh, what a beautiful Buddha!" I'll scream.' How many of you have been to Greece? Isn't it magnificent? People go to Greece, they go in the steps of St Paul, they see the buildings of all the pagan worship and they say, 'What wonderful architecture, what brilliant art!'

A Greek pastor friend of mine tells me nobody asks about the soul of Greece. They have probably the least gospel witness in the whole of Europe; it's frightening. But the apostle Paul looked at it and he was totally traumatized. As he saw all that there was in that great and magnificent city, he almost had a heart attack – that's what it literally means (verse 16). He shouted, not with the arrogance of a Christian who thinks he knows it all, but with the agony of seeing so much religion and so little – in fact, virtually no – getting through to the God who was there; and that, moving in his heart, led him to say, 'I have somehow got to get through to these people.' So what did he do? He went to the synagogue, but he also went to the market place and reasoned with them.

Do be careful, if you go on an evangelistic trip this summer, that you do actually talk with the people, and not just get them to pray without finding out what they think. A Hungarian Christian leader pleaded with me. 'Foreigners came over and they said 400 had made decisions to follow Christ. It took us such a long time and such a lot of work to follow them all up. We estimate there was one who became a Christian, and we praise the Lord for that. But we are rather concerned that where those people come from, they are saying that 400 became Christians.'

You see, Paul really took time to get close, to reason, to interact with what was really on the minds of these Athenian people. It took time. But I want you to notice, too, that as he saw all this religion, temples, altars and all the rest of it, it didn't shake his commitment to Jesus one whit.

Do you find sometimes that as you see all the Muslims on your campus, and perhaps even look in on their prayer meeting, and talk with them and you hear their testimonies as to how their religion works – do you find that you begin to think in those relativistic terms, where you say, 'Well, Christianity is true for me, but maybe that's true for them'? So you shake a bit, and you're not quite sure whether it's Jesus or nothing.

But Paul was sure. Confronted with all this religion he still holds, with his knees knocking like crazy as they certainly were when he went on to Corinth, to the claim that Jesus and the cross of Jesus are the answer that these religious people need.

But I want you to know this, too. As Paul began to reach out cross-culturally, he was determined to understand them. Notice that in Athens he didn't evangelize with his standard Jewish textbook on *How to Evangelize*. What does he do? He wants to understand these people. So he says, 'For as I walked around and looked carefully at your objects of worship' – he's asking himself, what makes these people tick? What do they really believe? How am I going to find a way into these people? – 'I even found an altar with this inscription: TO AN UNKNOWN GOD' (verse 23). There were altars to Zeus, to Uncle Tom Cobbleigh and all, but finally he found this particular altar and he thought: 'What a brilliant place to begin! They know there's a God whom they don't know, with whom they've got to get right.' Too right, they do! And he begins there.

As you read this sermon through, you find that Paul understood the Athenians' gut reaction. He read the books that they read, and they would have made your hair stand on end. He read them not just to be able to throw in the odd quotation, but to analyse them, to see if there was any way through to speak on these people's wavelengths, in language that jelled with the way that they were thinking.

It's very important to do that. My wife Rosemary once met a student evangelist who said, 'Brilliant! I just met a

Singaporean Buddhist who was only waiting to make a decision for Christ.' One of Rosemary's friends, a Singaporean professor, went to the hall of residence to check up on this 'decision for Christ'. The girl had placed an offering to Jesus on the god shelf. That's not Christian conversion, it's confusion, it's syncretism. Jesus doesn't accept being taken on board as an additional insurance policy. We are to turn from idols to serve the living and true God.

What is Paul doing? He is trying to understand people.

I heard a Brit talking to an African in Loughborough once, and the African eventually said, 'I can't talk to you any more.'

The Brit said, 'Why not?'

'You don't hear what I say.'

The Brit said, 'What do you mean?'

The African replied, 'You hear what you think that I ought to say, and you go on to the next point in your standard argument – but you don't hear what I say.'

They could never say that of Paul. He really wanted to get through. But I want you to notice that Luke tells us this story so that we understand that as we get on with evangelism, we've got to expect to be misunderstood. And Paul was misunderstood.

A foolish gospel

Verse 18: the gospel sounded *stupid* to the Athenians. 'What is this babbler trying to say?' They had their way of looking at life; it was miles away from Paul's. Some of them were Epicureans who believed that there was no purpose in life; that when you died there was nothing there; that the gods, if there were such things as gods, minded their own business, so you jolly well minded yours. But the most important thing about Epicureanism was self-fulfilment. That was all that mattered. Maybe some of you are secret Epicureans: all that really matters to you is that you enjoy yourself. That's not Christianity, it's Epicureanism.

Some were Stoics. They believed that there is a little bit of God in everything, that everything is God's will, that what will be will be and the most important thing for a Stoic is to do your duty. You learn to be self-sufficient, to stand on your own two feet. Then along comes Paul with his Christian gospel and they think he's absolutely potty. They call him a simpleton. 'How academically uninspiring!'

Are you prepared to be regarded as stupid?

A foreign gospel

The second thing you find is that they regarded the gospel as *foreign*. There is nothing more dismissive than to be told, as you work cross-culturally, that 'that's a foreign religion'. That's what the Athenians said: that it was what the Chinese communities would call 'of the foreign devil'. And it's very interesting that Paul uses half his sermon to explain that there is nothing foreign to the Athenians about the Christian gospel. Look how he does this in verse 24, and in verse 26 where he says, 'You may think that you are different from everybody else, but the fact of the matter is that you and I have a common ancestry. We are all descended from the one bloke, who made a muck of it.'

The Japanese think that Christianity is for foreigners. But you can say to a Japanese person, 'You do not have Adam on your ancestor tablet – but you should have.' Because we have the same common ancestry, we are in the same boat and share the same problem that all mankind has (verse 26). Then Paul says, 'God did this so that men would seek him and perhaps reach out for him and find him, though he is not far from each one of us' (verse 27). He has decided the length and the location of your life's journey and he's got a goal in it; this God wants you. This God, he says, wants you to seek him, to reach out and perhaps find him. He's not a foreign God.

And then Paul turns round at the end and says, 'Even your own poets have got a bit of an inkling about this: I found it as I read their books. It's not foreign. You are hankering after it even in Athenian culture' (*cf.* verse 28).

How many of you believe that the gospel belongs to the British? I asked some of the KGK staff, 'Do you believe that the gospel is authentically Japanese?' I found that came as a surprise to some of them. But it isn't a foreign religion. It is about a God who made them.

A confusing gospel

The gospel also sounded *confusing* to the Athenians. They said, 'Oh, there's a couple more gods on offer: Jesus and the resurrection. Jesus is the male one and the resurrection is the female one.'

Now, why on earth could they think like that? Have you ever noticed that you say something to somebody and it's obviously as clear as crystal to you and as clear as mud to the person you are talking to? Sometimes, of course, it's because we talk in the language of Zion, and they haven't done any language study so they can't understand it! But sometimes it's because they hear the gospel through their categories. The word 'grace' in the Philippines means going to mass, it always has done. The term 'born again' to a Buddhist is something he's trying to get out of, not something he wants to experience! And as I flew a few years ago into Japan on the airline whose adverts say that you can sit next to a sumo wrestler and still have enough room, they showed a video of the achievements of Japan; and there in the middle of it was this throwaway line – 'Japan's eight million gods are never far from the minds of their people.'

Then you begin your gospel presentation. 'God loves you and has a wonderful plan for your life.'

'Which god?'

'I've never thought about that . . . .'

But you need to, don't you? – because they will hear your statement through their grid. Paul, as he has begun to understand these Athenians, knows that their religious gut reaction is to build a temple, make an offering or design an image. And he says, 'No, no, no – that's not the way to do it.'

The world needs this sort of understanding evangelism. Don't commit yourself to three weeks' evangelism before you settle down. Give yourselves to understanding people so that you can apply the gospel until they grasp it.

A fascinating gospel

The gospel also sounded *fascinating* to the Athenians. They were the sort of people who said, 'Oh, how terribly interesting! We'll study that for a week or two until something else interesting comes up.' So Paul had to say to them, 'You listen, you lot have got to commit yourselves. God commands all people everywhere to repent.'

Paul's closing message

Now let me conclude. The sermon ends with three most important assertions that you must get a handle on tonight, and they all stem from this fact: the gospel was the most urgent need of the Athenians.

Just notice these wonderful truths that shine through this sermon.

People are meant to find God

See it there in verse 27: it's very important. 'God did this so that men would seek him and perhaps reach out for him and find him, though he is not far from each one of us.' Have you looked at crowds like that? I dodged between crowds in Beijing and wondered if they were going to mow me down. You can get a terribly negative attitude to hordes and hordes of people; and then you suddenly look at them again and think they are meant to find God. They may, like many students from China I've met here in Britain, say to you, 'I have never yet met a Christian' – but they are meant to find God. And there is yet more.

In the most godless place, God is near

You see what he says? 'He is not far from each one of us.' This is a place that is loaded with paganism; you would look at Athens and say, 'What a godless hole!' But Paul turns round and says, 'He's only a prayer away from each one of you, you know; he's keeping you going.'

As he wrote to the Italian Christians, in Romans 10:9, you've only got to trust God and talk to him, believe in your heart and confess with your lips; he's that near. There's no obstacle race to becoming a Christian. You've just got to trust him and talk to him. You've experienced that yourself, haven't you? At least, I hope you have; that all you had to do was trust him and talk to him. But somehow we do a mental flip when we look at foreigners, don't we? And we can't somehow believe, especially as (for example) we look at the Islamic world, that he is the one in whom they live and move and have their being.

They've only got to trust him and talk to him. It isn't actually an obstacle race and it's not that the place is totally godless. But there is a third thing that shines through this sermon.

People are not all right as they are

That is what I want to leave you with tonight. The Athenians are very wonderful in their city, but do you see what Paul says in verses 30 and 31? 'In the past God overlooked such ignorance' – your cock-eyed, extraordinary, unusual passion for all wrong religion – 'but now he commands all people everywhere to repent. For he has set a day when he will judge the world with justice by the man he has appointed.'

What does this mean? Does it mean that if people don't hear about God, God won't worry about their sin, he'll just overlook it? I don't think so. God didn't overlook the sin of the unevangelized in the time of the flood, did he? He took it deadly seriously.

I think that what it means is this: that Paul was saying to the Athenians, 'Up until now, God hasn't zapped you. You're still here. But that doesn't mean you can shrug your shoulders, because' (as he puts it in Romans 2:4) 'God's patience is meant to lead you to repentance.' Or, as Peter puts it in 2 Peter 3:9–10, 'The Lord is not slow in keeping his promise, as some understand slowness. He is patient with you, not wanting anyone to perish, but everyone to come to repentance. But the day of the Lord will come like a thief.'

And this is what he says here. All people everywhere need to be sorted out. They need to repent, because all people everywhere will stand before the Judge.

A man in Japan said to me, 'You missionaries are wasting your time; we Japanese people don't want to become Christians. You see, we don't like the Christian gospel because we Japanese achieve things; we don't need anybody to rescue us.'

I told him about a documentary I'd watched on television, where there was a massive fire in a hotel in Tokyo. And as the whole place was ablaze there was a man on a top window sill, hanging on by his fingernails. The fire engine came and they put up an enormous ladder; and you watched with amazement as a fireman climbed up, and up, and up, until eventually he got to him. And you were terrified: was he actually going to get him off this blazing building? Was it going to be all right? Somehow he managed to get the fellow over his shoulder and he brought him down this long, long ladder. When he got to the bottom there was a television reporter who turned to the man who had just been rescued and said, 'How does it feel?'

The man replied, 'It was terrifying. One slip and I would have fallen into hell.'

The odds are that he was exactly right. There are 121 million people in Japan who don't know Jesus. One slip . . . ! 'Up until now,' Paul said to them, 'God has not zapped you. Don't shrug your shoulders. It's time to repent, because people everywhere will have to come to terms with Jesus.'

And today, as you share the gospel in the Scriptures, people can know him as the rescuer that they need. Some sneered; some wanted to learn more, and a few were converted. God can use you like that if you're willing for the sneers, if you're prepared for the discussion, if you're ready to disciple people.

I pray that he will.

4

My place in God's plan

by Jonathan Lamb

Psalm 25

A short while ago I had to travel to Warsaw to visit the student movement in Poland. I was having some breakfast at London Heathrow waiting for the flight, and a man joined me at the table and began to talk. He was Polish, and was returning to Warsaw after being away for some fourteen years. He was going to visit his elderly mother there. Having been away for so long, he was asking me about my impressions of Poland, since I'd been there and a lot had changed in fourteen years. As we chatted, waiting for the flight, he told me a little about himself. He was working for Japanese Airlines and living in Australia.

As the conversation progressed, we got on to more personal matters. He spoke of his feelings of reticence about returning to his home country; of what had happened there, of what he would meet, of how his mother would be after fourteen years, of the uncertainties in his life. In the end he came out with one expression in this relatively short conversation, which said a great deal about him. He said, 'I have no idea who I am or where I belong.'

It wasn't just because he lived in Australia, flew Japanese Airlines and was Polish: it wasn't that kind of belonging that he was concerned about. It was more a deep-seated sense: 'I don't know where I am. I don't seem to have a sense of purpose and a destiny to my life.'

I think that if we speak to many of our college contemporaries, they will in their honest moments say much the same thing. They sense that there is somehow a deep inner trouble in their own lives. There doesn't seem to be a sense of direct purpose, of destiny. It is natural, in fact, that if God has placed eternity in our hearts then there is within us something that we find very difficult to bear, and that is, this sense of lostness. People who are made to be in a relationship with God, their creator and their redeemer, and who are outside of that relationship, inevitably feel this lack of direction. People try to find all sorts of substitutes for that relationship in order to plug the gap: substitutes for true hope in their lives.

Sometimes they attempt to maximize on their present experience; it's self-indulgence. Sometimes, for example, they look at astrology in an attempt to discover not only meaning for this present moment, but to find what may happen in the future.

Not long ago I read a newspaper article headed 'Career tips from the tarot cards'. It described business people in Wall Street, Manhattan, who in their lunch hour will visit 'The Gypsy Tea Kettle', where for $7 they can have a fifteen-minute discussion with a psychic or an astrologer. One such person, a businesswoman in her mid-thirties, was quoted as saying, 'Psychics are more valuable than friends. They can see where you are going and they can give you hope for the future.'

People want to feel that they matter, that they belong, that their lives have some kind of significance, that they are moving towards something – that there is some kind of destiny.

I was interested to read the closing paragraph of a book by a mathematician and scientist, Paul Davies, whose writing some of you will know. It is called *The Mind Of God: Science and the Search for Ultimate Meaning*, and it deals with the new physics. In a very revealing statement he says,

> I cannot believe that our existence in this universe is a mere quirk of fate, an accident of history, an incidental blip in the great cosmic drama. Our involvement is too intimate . . . . Through conscious beings the universe has generated self-awareness. This can be no trivial detail, no minor product of mindless, purposeless forces. We are truly meant to be here.[1]

1. Paul Davies, *The Mind of God* (Penguin, 1993), p. 232.

Now the Christian believer, of all people, is described in the New Testament as a person full of hope, as a person who is in touch with the God who brought him into being, who has redeemed him, who holds this universe in his hands; the God who knows the end from the beginning. So there is a plan not only for me as an individual but for this entire universe. This world is not heading for the dust bowls of infinity. There is a plan and God is behind it; and because I have trusted in God the creator and the redeemer, I too as an individual fit into his plan. Yet surprisingly, when you talk to Christians, there is a great crisis of confidence about that very idea: my place in God's plan, the sense of purpose in my life.

Let me read to you something that appeared in a publication from IVCF (the American equivalent of UCCF). 'If there is a serious concern among Christian students today it is for guidance. Holiness may have been the passion of another generation's Christian young men and women, or soul winning, or evangelizing the world, but not today. Today the theme is getting to know the will of God.'[1] And I don't know how you feel about this subject, but there is a rising anxiety level among many Christians over it. We long to be certain about God's plan for our lives. We are fearful about making some kind of mistake, so that somehow we enter God's second best instead of what God really intends for us.

There is a strange, if well-motivated, anxiety growing. As Jim Packer puts it in one of his books, 'Anxious people become vulnerable to strange influences and do zany things.'[2] And they do: people look for all kinds of signals and omens, all kinds of irrational hunches which might somehow give them a clue to what God is saying to them, how God is leading them, their place in God's plan. And for many of us as we grow older as Christians, we have a sneaking suspicion that in fact (to use a well-known phrase) God loves us, and everybody else has a wonderful plan for

1. Quoted in J. I. Packer, *Laid-Back Religion* (IVP, 1987), p. 71.
2. *Ibid.*, p. 72.

our lives. It somehow seems that we are called upon to do this and that – but what am I *meant* to do, what is *God's* plan for my life?

Well, discovering my place in God's plan needs to be seen in the context of one great privilege: *knowing God the guide*. For the Bible's emphasis is more on the guide than on the issue of guidance. It says more about what God is able to do in our lives as guide, teacher, sovereign Lord and shepherd, than it does about the details or mechanics of how he is going to lead us. And so to place guidance in a box somehow separate from the rest of our Christian life is to engage in a very dangerous kind of compartmentalization. It is not a separate issue. Knowing my place in God's plan and knowing God are inseparable.

So for just for a few minutes, from these verses in Psalm 25, I want to highlight two privileges which every Christian believer here and around the world enjoys, and then conclude with three basic conditions for discovering God's purpose for our own lives.

David's song, as we can see from this psalm, is built around a fundamental expression of his trust in the Lord. He's surrounded by various pressures – his enemies, his guilt. But also (in verses 4–5) he deals most particularly with his desire to discover God's ways, God's purposes. And that's going to be our focus.

God has a plan for our lives

The first privilege is very straightforward. It is that God does have a plan for our lives. In fact, the psalmist presupposes it in all his requests. Look at their frequency: verse 4, 'Show me your ways, O LORD, teach me your paths'; verse 5, 'Guide me in your truth and teach me'; verse 8, 'He instructs sinners in his ways'; verse 9, 'He guides the humble in what is right and teaches them his way'; verse 12, 'He will instruct him in the way chosen for him.'

Let's look at the force of the repetition in the structure of David's song (which in fact is built around the Hebrew alphabet), which constantly affirms God's way, God's paths, God's purposes. Verse 8, it is because of *who God* is that he will lead those who trust him. Because of the Lord's goodness and faithfulness (verse 10), he will reveal his ways and his purposes. It's important to see David's emphasis in his song: verse 8, 'He instructs sinners in his ways.' He is guiding us (verse 9) into what is right.

So God's overall goal for our lives, if you want a simple answer, is a *moral goal*. His concern is the kind of people we should be, which is far more important than the kind of activities we should do.

And that's exactly the emphasis in the New Testament. Guidance for us is very often a matter of 'What should I do?' For example, 'Whom should I marry? *Should* I marry?' But the Bible tends to concentrate much more on this over-arching purpose that God has for our lives. There is exactly the same emphasis in Romans 8:28–29, which states that God has a plan and then tells us what that plan is for our lives: 'We know that in all things God works for the good of those who love him, who have been called according to his purpose. For those God foreknew he also predestined' – what? – 'to be conformed to the likeness of his Son, that he might be the firstborn among many brothers.'

So God's concern, his plan, for our lives is for the *whole* of our lives. When we're discussing the subject of guidance we tend to think of the big vocational choices: what kind of job I should do, how I should use my time, whether or not I should get married and if so to whom.

It's understandable, for these things shape our lives so decisively. But when you look at this New Testament passage you find here too that God's overarching concern is to make us more like Jesus. It is his primary goal. He's not chiefly concerned with guiding us over just one decision.

If tonight you're thinking of one issue about which you long that God will guide you – well, he may graciously do so; but he's much more concerned about the type of person you're going to be. He doesn't just want to move in and merely decorate the kitchen, he wants to decorate the whole house. He wants to take over the whole of our lives. It is a theme frequently reflected in the biblical writers and one picked out frequently by Paul. 'We are God's workmanship, created in Christ Jesus to do good works, which God prepared in advance for us to do' (Eph. 2:10). He already has this in mind for you and for me. He's already prepared it, even before eternity, and because it is God's plan it is good and perfect. So there is nothing to be feared about God's plan in our lives.

Sometimes people talk about 'surrendering' to the will of God, and that's a useful and biblical idea. But the problem is that it implies that we're kicking and screaming, that God has finally got hold of us and we say, 'OK! I give up! I surrender!'

Paul Little once wrote that people imagine that God is peering over the balcony of heaven trying to find anybody who is enjoying life; and that when he sees a happy person he yells, 'Cut that out!'[1] It's an almost blasphemous concept of God. His purpose for us is good and perfect. His plan for our lives has been shaped in eternity and the guide himself knows what is best for us.

That's the most important thing. God has a plan for our lives. It is what the New Testament terms his call. He is concerned about everybody in this auditorium, everybody on the globe, who is called to know Jesus Christ. So when people ask you, 'What is your calling?' the first answer must be, 'I am called to belong to God. I'm called to belong to Jesus.'

And if this moral transformation is taking place in our lives, then, as Psalm 25 assures us, the Lord will be able to instruct us. He will be able to guide us in those details which doubtless we have on our minds; he will lead us in the way he has chosen for us; he will be able to use us wherever he has placed us, if that moral transformation is taking place and we are becoming more like Jesus. That's his plan for our lives.

God promises us his presence

Some years ago, I was driving to find an international camp site in what was then East Germany. It was a Sunday night

1. Paul Little, *Day by Day Guidance* (Falcon, 1976), p.13.

and we were driving through the lanes; it was getting darker and darker; the petrol gauge on the van was dropping lower and lower, and in those days you were only allowed to stay in official camp sites; you couldn't park on the roadside. So we had to find the camp site. We'd just crossed the border and hadn't changed our currency and we were running out of petrol. We decided we'd have to ask somebody for directions. I spoke to somebody in my rather poor German, and he replied, 'Yes, sure! You go left, left, right, right; you go straight across the bridge; you go right at the hotel; you go third right, after the second set of traffic lights; you turn left, you go straight on, you're there . . . .'

So we got back into the van and did our very best to find the site. It was no good at all; my German couldn't cope with those instructions. So we asked somebody else, and again the same kind of complex instructions. Then eventually, with the petrol gauge sinking and the night blackening, we stopped a couple in the street and asked them. They said, 'Hang on,' and jumped into the van. They took us straight there.

Having a guide is so much better than guidance, isn't it? – having somebody who says, 'I will get in with you and travel with you.' That is what makes all the difference to this business of discovering the plan of God. God hasn't given us a book of rules. He is not like some kind of celestial computer, spewing out a printout like a travel agent's itinerary, of all of the things that you've got to do, and you know that if you miss the train connection or arrive late for check-in at the airport, that's it: you've blown it. That's not the biblical picture of guidance at all. The whole business of discovering God's purpose in my life, my place in his plan, has to do with the fact that he is a companion who is making the journey with us.

You find that frequently in David's writings. You see it in Psalm 25, which is full of that kind of confidence. Verse 5: 'Guide me . . . for you are God my Saviour.' Verse 9: 'He guides . . . [he] teaches . . .'; or if you want a wonderful expression of intimacy, look at verse 14: 'The LORD confides in those who fear him.' David is saying, 'The Lord himself is our guide, our leader, our teacher.' He says exactly the same kind of thing in Psalm 32, where in verse 8 you find a very beautiful image: 'I will instruct you and teach you in the way you should go; I will counsel you and watch over you.' Or, as one version puts it, 'I will counsel you with my eye upon you.'

I would be a very strange father if, when my youngest daughter began to progress from crawling to taking her first steps, I'd said, 'Well, off you go, Anna, have a crack at the Pennine Way.' That's not the parents' role in helping children to walk. They're there, they're watching the crockery and the china and everything else, but they're watching and supporting the child very carefully. They're alongside, they're guiding. 'With my eye upon you I will instruct you and teach in the way you should go.' That is how the Lord acts.

That was what was important for Moses, do you remember? He wanted to know his place in God's plan. He wanted to know God's ways. He wanted to see God's glory. So when he made those bold requests to God, the assurance that he received was: 'My Presence will go with you, and I will give you rest' (Ex. 33:14). And Jesus, when he was explaining this issue of discovering God's will and purpose for our lives in terms of the shepherd image, said, 'My sheep listen to my voice; I know them, and they follow me' (Jn. 10:27).

In a very good recent book by Phillip Jensen and Tony Payne modestly entitled *The Last Word on Guidance*,[1] the principle is slightly overstated, but that is no bad thing: *The first step towards understanding God's guidance is to understand the guiding God*. To know what God is like, how God thinks, what motivates God himself, what the plans are of the guide himself; and most of all, to know this certainty and this assurance that the guide himself is with us. There is at that point a special security, a special confidence.

It would be no surprise to me if there were hundreds at

1. Phillip D. Jensen and Tony Payne, *The Last Word on Guidance* (ANZEA Books, St Matthias Press, 1991).

this conference who are a little bewildered about what's happening to them. Something may have happened in your family, in your life, in your studies, or in some kind of relationship. And you wonder, what on earth is God doing? Or you're thinking about the future; you've studied and you've graduated and there seems no clear way for to use the gifts which God has given you; and you're bewildered, you're very uncertain about this whole business of 'your place in God's plan'. You see other people apparently succeeding and being fulfilled, but somehow God seems to have passed you by.

Well, I want to say especially to you that this great privilege is very important to grasp. The guide is our companion. He is himself getting into the car and saying, 'I am travelling this road with you. You may not know what's ahead. You may be very uncertain, even bewildered, about what's happening, but I am with you.'

Another psalm of David, the well-known Psalm 23, affirms precisely these two privileges. 'The LORD is my shepherd' – the Lord is with me, he is providing for me. And where is he leading me? He leads me 'in paths of righteousness'. There it is. He has a moral goal, a moral plan for our lives. He has a plan for our lives, and he promises us his presence.

Three basic conditions

As we conclude, let us turn to three basic conditions that emerge from David's writing in Psalm 25 about how to discern the will of God and our place in God's plan.

Pure motives

If we've come here serious in our desire that God should use us, that we should find ourselves right at the centre of God's plan for our lives, then there is a very important exercise that you and I have to conduct in God's presence. We must allow him to search our hearts. We must allow him to test our motives every day, because we're continually under pressure to conform to the world of which we are a part. As we think about our lives, our future, our role, we're bombarded by ideas about status and about position and about money and about possessions; about career advancements, about life in the fast lane; about the urgent need to have a boyfriend, a girlfriend, a partner. All the time this bombardment from secular media, and even from people with whom we live in our flats and our halls of residence, continually insists: 'This is the type of person you should be, this is the type of job you should get, this is the type of person you need on your arm.'

Well, Paul – writing about his own basic motivation – said something very simple in 2 Corinthians 5:9 – 'We make it our goal to please him.' Making it our goal to please him becomes an important filter on all of our decisions, namely, what are the Lord's priorities? 'Seek first his kingdom and his righteousness' (Mt. 6:33).

I remember some years ago reading about someone who was a student in 1906 at Imperial College in London. His name was James Fraser. Another student passed him a leaflet that completely transformed his life, most particularly because it challenged his motivation. His biographer remarks that 'Fraser knew that his field of study – engineering – held immense prospects world-wide, and that his own ability was considerable. But the booklet struck at the very root of his assumptions. It spoke of losing one's life for Christ's sake, of dying in order to live; in short, of renouncing obvious plans and prospects because God had something better.'[1]

Fraser's biographer described how, in God's presence, the Lord used some simple words in that booklet to cut at some of his assumptions, motives, and ideas about his career and relationships. It was the beginning of a series of events in his life that were to lead to a lifetime's service in mission in China. 'Delight yourself in the Lord,' Psalm 37 says, 'and he will give you the desires of your heart.'

David wrote Psalm 25 in the awareness of his own failure. Several times he asks the Lord for forgiveness, for example

1. Eileen Crossman, *Mountain Rain: A New Biography of James Fraser* (OMF, 1982), pp. 3-4.

in verses 7 and 11. And as he searches his heart and examines his motives, as he looks at his life in the Lord's presence, he realizes how far short he has fallen from God's standards and how much he has to do in this whole business of achieving God's moral purpose. I do not think it is a mistake that those appeals for forgiveness sit alongside David's appeal for the Lord's guidance, his appeal that the Lord would show him his ways. It is fundamental to being used by God in his plan for our lives that we should be cleansed from sin, that we should be led by the Spirit and that we should learn this humble holiness. Verse 9: 'He teaches [the humble] his way.' And if by the Spirit's help we have that kind of passion for holiness, we will then, in our lives, be able to distinguish what the Lord is saying to us from our own impure motives and desires.

That is what David is saying in verses 10 and 12. He realizes that he needs to have his motives out in the open before the Lord. I'm inviting you to do that tonight; bring up to the surface, into God's presence, your motivation and your thinking about the future, offering to him what you have and asking, 'Lord, forgive me, cleanse me, give me a passion first for you, for your holiness.' And then as you delight yourself in the Lord, he'll give you the desires of your heart.

Renewed minds

One of the best-known passages in the New Testament about discovering God's will is Romans 12:1–2: 'Do not conform any longer to the pattern of this world,' – that's the first condition, pure motives – 'but be transformed by the renewing of your mind. Then you will be able to test and approve what God's will is – his good, pleasing and perfect will.'

So Paul is saying that instead of the world's values shaping your life and how you want to use what God has given you, God's truth must be the deciding factor. That is the only way in which we'll be able to discern accurately God's will for our lives. We develop a framework for our own thinking, and therefore for our behaviour, by which we can judge the information we receive. It allows us to take particular decisions, whether major or minor, in a way that is perfectly consistent with God's truth: renewed minds.

Look at Psalm 25, how David appeals for that kind of instruction. Verse 4, 'Teach me your paths'; verse 5, 'Guide me in your truth and teach me'; verse 8, 'He instructs sinners in his ways.' It's even clearer if we go back to Psalm 32, verses 8–9; again the promise that the Lord would lead, that there would be guidance, that we will discover God's plan. It's threefold. 'I will instruct you and teach you in the way you should go; I will counsel you with my eye upon you.'

But how is the Lord going to do that for David? How will he fulfil his promises to you and me, to lead us, to teach us, to counsel us? Verse 9: 'Do not be like the horse or the mule, which have no understanding but must be controlled by bit and bridle or they will not come to you.' God will show us our place in his plan, he will lead us, he'll show us the way to go – but it won't be by force; force is for animals. It will be by intelligence. You see, God is saying, 'You're not a mule; I've given you understanding. It's a God-given gift. And I'm going to guide you through that.'

It won't be through irrational 'hunches'. It's going to be through a renewed mind that is exposed to God's word, the living word, which we're rejoicing in here at Word Alive. That's how he'll guide us.

You may know the story of the young man at a missionary training college. Nearing the end of his course he longed to know his place in God's plan and what part of the world he should serve in. As he walked along the street he thought, 'Well, I'll look in the shop windows, and if the first thing I see suggests anything, maybe that's how the Lord wants to guide me.' In the first shop, sure enough he saw some Brazil nuts. It must be Brazil! He went to his lecturer in the college and said, 'The Lord's finally told me where I should serve him!'

'Oh? Where's that?'

'Brazil! I saw some Brazil nuts in a shop window.'

The lecturer replied, 'It's a good job you didn't see a Mars bar!'

People do have all kinds of irrational ideas about how God is going to lead them. 'I really could do with a girlfriend' – so you scan through Scripture and there it is: 'Go out with Joy.'

But David says, 'You are not like a mule. It's not irrational impulses, hunches, waiting for the next blue car to go by – all the devices people dream up to discover God's purpose for their lives.' If this privilege is true, that the guide is with us, then increasingly he's going to transform our minds so that we then can determine his good purposes for us. As we submit our minds, our thinking and our understanding to him, as they are transformed, as we think as he thinks, then this kind of godly wisdom will be the most significant factor in knowing God's plan day by day.

There's a wonderful verse that I think should be the text for this gathering. It's 1 Thessalonians 2:13, where Paul describes God's word as something living, which goes on working in those who go on believing. It's not academic, it's not distant or cold, 'out there'. God's word is 'going on working in those who go on believing', shaping your mind and mine, giving us understanding. That's the way to discover how the Lord is going to lead us day by day.

And it leads me, finally, to the third condition that emerges loud and clear from this psalm.

Complete trust

The passage in Romans 12 that we looked at explains that if we are going to discover God's good, pleasing and perfect will, then in addition to pure motives and renewed minds we need a total consecration of ourselves, the whole of our lives given to his service. 'I urge you, brothers, in view of God's mercy, to offer your bodies as living sacrifices, holy and pleasing to God – this is your reasonable act of worship' (verse 1, NIV margin).

Do you see? That's why tonight's theme follows hard on the heels of what we've already had in these celebrations. We've been thinking about these great themes of justification; God's purpose in the Lord Jesus Christ of restoring people like you and me who were lost, who were God's enemies, hopeless in a hopeless and fractured world. He's not only forgiven us, he's transformed us to become like Jesus. We're members of his family. And Paul says, in the light of God's mercy to you, because of what God has done, I appeal to you: present your bodies as living sacrifices, consecrate yourselves to God; give everything that you have to him.

That's the way to discover God's plan for your life. It's that kind of surrender, that kind of complete trust.

The basic attitude in David's writing in Psalm 25 is exactly that. What lies behind his appeal to understand God's ways and God's guidance? Look at verse 2: 'In you I trust, O my God'; his absolute, exclusive trust in the guide. Verse 5, 'My hope is in you all day long'; verse 20, 'I take refuge in you'; verse 21, 'My hope is in you.'

Now how could David say all that? Why was he so confident?

He was under pressure. His life may have been at stake. He was feeling the pressure of enemies. He felt his own sinfulness, that's for sure. But David was absolutely confident that he could trust God wholly. And the reason is that he understood something about the guide. Verse 5, he understood God's saving power; verse 6, he understood God's steadfast love; verses 9 and 10, he understood God's goodness and God's justice; verse 10, he understood God's faithfulness.

At the human level, whom do you trust? I once had a go at abseiling. Have you ever tried it? It involves going over a cliff backwards – not a lot of fun! It was on a cliff in Scotland, the only time I've ever done it, and the person at the top of the cliff paying out the rope was a very good friend of mine. Now, I knew that he had a great sense of humour, but I also knew him very well. And the reason I was willing to go over the top was that I knew the person who was holding the rope. I was absolutely sure that this guy – despite his zany sense of humour! – would make sure that everything was all right.

We trust people whom we know. The more we know them, the more we understand them. The human analogy, of course, has its limitations, but for us believers and for David, the condition is absolutely clear. The reason he could seek God's ways and ask that God would lead him was established on this foundation of complete trust, of consecration to do God's will. He knew this God, he knew the guide. Verse 9 – it's the humble whom God will guide, who display not the stubbornness of a mule but the willing and intelligent response of a sinner who has found God's grace.

Those of us who have found God's grace have been lifted out of emptiness and hopelessness and brought into his family. So we need now to surrender our lives to him. Of course, that means being willing to trust him for what lies in the future. That's a problem for most of us. Many of us pray, 'Lord, show me your will – and then I can decide whether or not it fits in with what I have in mind.' If only God would allow us just to lift the curtain a little bit and discover what is on the other side, then we could decide whether or not we really wanted to trust him. But it doesn't work like that, does it? This unconditional surrender, this trust, is built on the fact that God's plan for us is good and perfect.

Do you believe it? God's will for you is good and perfect. If you believe that, then you're ready to accept it, because you trust the guide. Are you ready for that kind of commitment, that total consecration?

I spoke not long ago to a young man who was applying to a Christian organization and I asked him what it was that was leading him to go into full-time Christian work. He thought for a moment, then said, 'Well, basically I want to be financially secure and I want to travel the world.'

When you listen to someone say that, you realize not only how selfish is the motivation, but actually how unrealistic is the expectation about serving God – as some of the UCCF staff will tell you! It's unrealistic because, if you're going to do this, if you're going to consecrate yourself completely to serve God now where he's placed you – unemployed, student, doctor, vet, teacher, social worker, industrialist, business person, housewife – if God's going to use you, it may well cost you everything you have. So this business of trust and complete surrender isn't some kind of game.

Yet on the other hand, there is no other place to be for us Christians, is there? – because he is the safest guide in the universe. As Hudson Taylor put it, it's not so much a matter of our great faith but of faith in a great God. We are to be roped to that safest guide.

Let me read to you some words as I draw to a close, spoken by William McConnell, a believer who was Deputy Governor of the Maze Prison in Northern Ireland. He was assassinated. Shortly before he was killed, he wrote these words:

> I have committed my life, my talents, my work, my action, to Almighty God in the sure and certain knowledge that however slight my hold on him may have been, his promises are sure. His hold on me is complete.

And I say to you, brothers and sisters, as I say to myself, we need have no doubt that God does have a plan for our lives, and that God himself will be alongside us on that journey. We need have no doubt that it is a good and a perfect plan, and he will show us day by day what it is that he wants us to do.

But the real issue of tonight's session, the main question, is this. Do I really want to fulfil his plan? Am I wholly available to the Lord? Am I willing to trust him with everything that I have?

As David sought to discover God's plan for his life, he not only knew that God could be trusted; he committed his life to that guide.

5

Our confidence in God

by Lindsay Brown

Daniel 3

This address was preceded by one by Sir Norman Anderson on Hebrews 11, in which he spoke movingly of his personal experience of bereavement – a theme that Lindsay Brown picks up a number of times in the address that follows. (See also p. 143.)

I am thirty-nine years of age. I've never been afraid of anybody (maybe because I grew up on a council housing estate in South Wales where they breed them quite tough). At least, that was the case till two months ago – and then I visited Peru. And for the first time in my life I experienced real fear.

I was just about to leave for Peru when I saw the news of the elections in the capital, Lima, where quite a number of politicians were killed by Maoist guerrillas. When I arrived I found that the mayor of the little village where we were having our conference had been shot on the doorstep three days earlier. I heard that they were targeting evangelical Christians; 300 ministers or pastors had been executed in the last twelve years, deliberately sought out by the Maoist guerrilla movement Sendero Luminoso. Some foreign missionaries had also been shot. I was worried. I said to the Regional Secretary for Latin America, 'I'm a good target for a kidnap – I've got red hair, I work with an international student organization.' He replied, 'Lindsay, Sendero don't kidnap people, they shoot them!'

I thought about my family. Maybe I was prepared to meet with the Lord if that were his choice, but what about my wife and son? We have already lost a daughter. It would be crushing for them to be left on their own without a father and husband. So I prayed for the Lord to preserve me.

Things got worse. In the building in which I stayed the bedroom window had been broken by a nearby bomb-blast a few days earlier. They took me on a seven-hour bus ride, over 14,000 ft up into the High Sierras. We stayed in a conference centre that hadn't been used for a year because of the violence. The students hired it because it cost only $3 a day. I discovered that the conference centre was 9 miles from the headquarters of Sendero. Afterwards students drove me to catch the bus back down the mountain, and I hid behind a cardboard box in the back. I was certainly glad to get home.

Some of the students coming to the conference actually travelled by bus through a valley on one side of which were the guerrillas, and on the other the army. They came through the cross-fire to the conference. I talked with one young female student who was only twenty-one and had been a Christian for two and a half years. She was studying sociology. She asked me what I thought of sociology. I mumbled that it was a useful subject to study. Then I said, 'Why do you ask?'

'Well,' she said, 'all the male sociology undergraduates in my department are members of Sendero. When I became a Christian I was petrified by them. They put a list up on the notice board in the university Students Union of the people they were going to shoot, then they ticked them off one by one as they killed them. I thought, "What will happen to me?" I was fearful for eighteen months,' she said. 'Then last summer I determined that whatever they do to me, I must share the gospel, because it's true.'

I was rebuked. As I experienced this fear for the first time, I thought: how can my faithfulness in the Lord be restored? Then I thought of Shadrach, Meshach and Abednego.

The theme of this evening is 'Our confidence in God', moving from fearfulness to faithfulness. And as I read this chapter again in Peru, I thought of three reasons why these three men refused to be fearful before Nebuchadnezzar, and became faithful. And I would like to share them with you this evening.

The first is this.

They recognized the sovereign power of God

They recognized him as the Lord of heaven and over all the earth and the universe. This is a prominent thread running through the elaborate tapestry of the prophecy of Daniel. You see it in 1:2, where at the time of the exile the young Jews were taken to Babylon. The reference is to the fact that it was the sovereign Lord who gave Jehoiakim, king of Judah, into the hand of Nebuchadnezzar. Later on in the chapter we see that God caused the chief official to show favour and sympathy to Daniel (verse 9); he and his friends were elevated to a senior position, and given authority in the kingdom.

In chapter 2 we have the account of how the king had a dream. He went to all his astrologers. None of them could help him to interpret it, so he went to Daniel. Daniel was able to interpret it, but notice some of his language. In the dream a great statue with a golden head and feet of clay symbolized King Nebuchadnezzar's greatness, but also his weakness. As Daniel explained the dream he said to him (verse 37), 'You, O king, are the king of kings. The God of heaven has given you dominion and power and might and glory.' God had given him that authority and this glory; but Daniel goes on in verses 44–45 to say, 'In the time of those kings, the God of heaven will set up a kingdom that will never be destroyed' (after Nebuchadnezzar's kingdom has ended), and that kingdom will not 'be left to another people. The great God has shown the king what will take place in the future.' So there is a thread running through.

Then in chapter 3, in which Nebuchadnezzar seems to have forgotten this encounter with the God of heaven who works in his life, and whom he praises at the end of chapter 2, he sets up a golden image – maybe because of the jealousy of some of his counsellors – and asks people to worship at it. Shadrach, Meshach and Abednego, friends of Daniel, refused to do so. Nebuchadnezzar calls them before him, ready to throw them into the fiery furnace. But they speak to him the stark words of verses 17 and 18, which again focus on the sovereignty of God. 'If we are thrown into the blazing furnace, the God we serve is able to save us from it, and he will rescue us from your hand, O king. But even if he does not, we want you to know, O king, that we will not serve your gods or worship the image of gold you have set up.'

They believed that the God of heaven was sovereign over the whole universe. You can see it in these first three chapters. A great Dutch theologian at the beginning of this century emphasized this; his name was Abraham Kuyper, a theologian, pastor, and Prime Minister of the Netherlands. Kuyper, referring to this passage, says, 'There is not in the total expanse of human life a single square inch of which God, who alone is sovereign, does not declare, "That is mine."' And that's why Christian students should seek to apply their Christian minds, and Christian truth as found in the Scriptures, to all areas of life.

But, this passage teaches us, this God who is sovereign over all the universe was concerned for the personal circumstances of these people. They were children of the king of the universe; nothing was outside of his control, and he could intervene.

I'm reminded of the story of a General Secretary of the Vietnamese student movement whom I met last summer. His name was Chong. In 1975, when the Americans flew many Vietnamese pastors and believers out of the country, he decided to stay. The first Sunday after the Americans left he started a little church in Saigon with some students. It grew to a thousand people over ten years. Then Chong was arrested and spent several years in solitary confinement. He was released just two years ago in 1991 and thrown out of the country, partly because so many prisoners had become Christians through his witness.

Once, Chong was being interviewed by soldiers. They said to him 'Don't you realize what we can do to you?'

Chong responded with these powerful words: 'It is God who brought me to this prison, and if he wants me to stay here I will. But if God wants me to be freed from this prison I will be freed, and there is nothing in heaven or earth that you can do to stop it.' And of course he was; because the God of the universe was interested in his personal circumstances.

I want to apply this focus on the sovereignty of God, which is a foundational Christian truth, because some of you last night offered yourselves to a life of service before the Lord. But you will take knocks later on in life, and if you don't understand that God is sovereignly in control, not only of the universe but of your daily circumstances and of your life, breath by breath and day by day, then you will be cast away with the wind. It's a vital Christian doctrine.

My first application is that this passage indicates that *God is concerned not only for the fiery-furnace experiences of life but also for the small details*. He is concerned about our academic lives. He is concerned for our relationships with our parents, and that will be important for some of us when we return home, for some of us will experience the fiery furnace of parental hostility. A student I know went to a conference like this some years ago. She went home thrilled, telling her parents what a wonderful experience she had had. Her mother said, 'Don't ever mention the name of Jesus Christ again in this house.'

You may not have that experience – but you might, for it does happen to some believers. But we must understand that God is sovereignly in control, even in those circumstances. Sometimes I think he gives us the parents we have, to show us how unloving and hard is our heart before we reach out to others.

A second application: this passage indicates that *the believer, who is a servant of the Lord, is not promised that life will be trouble-free*. I mentioned that 300 pastors have been executed in Peru in the last twelve years. Most of them were Pentecostals, who believe in miraculous events. Professor Anderson has talked to us about Hebrews 11, which on the one hand talks about people who are supernaturally delivered, and on the other – and almost in the same breath – about some who were faithful, and served the Lord, but were sawn in two or were stoned. Sometimes such things happen even to the believer, and we can't always understand why. All we can say is that in the case of Shadrach, Meshach and Abednego they had an eternal perspective. They said, 'Well, if God doesn't deliver us we still won't yield to the god you asked us to worship.' Why? Because they knew that death was not the end.

In a very real sense, we are living on Easter Saturday, between Good Friday and the fulfilment of the hope of glory in heaven. A Russian physicist, Sergei Terrasenko, spoke of 'God's cosmic perspective'. You and I often understand things in terms of how they affect us immediately, but God sees things from a different perspective. He looks down from heaven and sees how events occurring in our lives are preparing us to become more faithful and effective as witnesses, and ultimately preparing us to become more like the Lord Jesus Christ, with this eventual fulfilment which will be in heaven.

So life is not promised to be trouble free, even for the full-time Christian servant, the person who gives himself or herself whole-heartedly to serving the Lord.

Next, I think, this passage highlights the fact that *if we believe God is sovereign, fidelity is important*. I always remember, when my daughter was dying in hospital, my wife coming home and saying to me, 'Lindsay, the angels are watching us.' There is a cosmic world out there, about which we know very little. God sees what is happening, and he sees our reactions. He is watching how we behave. And there is a devil who watches how we behave. There are angels in heaven who watch, and there are fallen angels in hell who watch. Fidelity and the reaction of the believer are important. Francis Schaeffer once wrote a book about this, entitled *The Church Before the Watching World*. Even when we don't understand why things may happen to us, we are still to remain faithful to the sovereign God.

Caleb was one of the graduates of the student movement in Peru. He had received two death threats. He was a staff worker with IFES and also led the Evangelical Alliance in Peru. I said to him, 'Caleb, do you ever feel like leaving the country?' He had two daughters, aged seven and nine; I was thinking of their plight if their parents were killed. He replied, 'Lindsay, my wife and I have talked about it. But you know, we really believe God is sovereign. We have given our lives into his hands. If he wants us to live, then we will live; and if he chooses to take us to be with himself, we must be ready. But if we leave the country we believe it will be devastating for the church. For if the leaders leave, what example will that be to the rest of the church?'

How often do you hear that today? Very often we want the soft option, the easy way out. But the testimony of Shadrach, Meshach and Abednego is fidelity before the sovereign God of the universe, who watches how we behave when faced by temptations and trials in life.

Then, I think, this passage hints at the fact that *some things are a mystery*. We cannot always understand why God allows some things to happen in our lives. Professor Anderson hinted that he didn't fully understand why he has lost three children. I confess to you, I don't fully understand why my daughter was taken. We prayed for her healing, we anointed her with oil, we prayed our hearts out. But in the providence of God, he chose to take her. I don't fully understand. But I do know that it's not the end, and I share King David's belief: that I will meet her beyond the grave, just as David knew he would meet his child there (2 Sa. 12:23).

One more thing about sovereignty. It's necessary to hold in juxtaposition, in tension, the sovereignty of God and the goodness of God. There were eighteenth-century philosophers who had a deist concept of God as one who set the world in motion, like a Swiss clock-maker, and then let it run, disinterestedly, without much interest in individuals. The Muslim view of God, in many ways, is of a God who is impersonal and distant, who does not speak of loving us. But the Christian revelation of God is unique. It speaks of a God who is sovereign, who is Lord of heaven and earth, who loves of his own accord his individual creations.

When I first came across the writings of John Calvin I remember writing to a friend in Beirut and saying, 'Hugh, I have realized that I am a slave of Christ.' He wrote back, 'If that's all you think you are, you are no different from a Muslim. You are not just a slave, you are also a son.'

That's the distinction of the Christian. It doesn't mean

that we always understand why some things will happen in our human experience, when knocks may occur in the future. But we must hold that in tension with the sovereign God, who sees from heaven and ordains. We are not in a universe in chaos which is driven by chance, but one driven by a God who guides, rules, sustains, upholds and directs – but who also is touched by our infirmities, as he says to Isaiah the prophet (*cf*. Is. 63:9).

This is the first lesson that we need to heed from the story of Shadrach, Meshach and Abednego, a foundation for you if you want to move from being fearful to faithful – trust in the sovereign Lord of the universe in case tidal waves of disappointment come your way in the future. Hold on to God as the sovereign Lord who loves you, or you'll be tossed to and fro.

They knew the presence of God

In these circumstances they were thrown into the fire. In verse 25, we see that Nebuchadnezzar was shocked when he saw someone who was like the Son of God (son of gods, some translations read). I believe it was the pre-incarnate person of the Lord Jesus Christ who was meeting with them and was present with them.

Of course the New Testament, in 1 Peter, tells us that just as these people were in exile, so we believers in this era are also exiles in this world, waiting to return to our home, as it were, in heaven (*cf*. 1 Pet. 2:11). And we have a promise: the presence of God, as they experienced it there.

Three applications.

First, this passage highlights the fact that *the God of the universe is present with us when we are passing through tribulations*. We are not alone. They must have known the psalm of David, Psalm 139, which puts it beautifully, powerfully and poetically: 'Where can I go from your Spirit? Where can I flee from your presence? If I go up to the heavens, you are there; if I make my bed in the depths, you are there. If I rise on the wings of the dawn, if I settle on the far side of the sea, even there your hand will guide me, your right hand will hold me fast' (Ps. 139:7–10).

David knew the presence of God. Those who suffer for Christ have the promise of his presence with them, even in the most fiery of furnaces.

I will never forget the testimony of the great evangelist of the Chinese student movement in the 1950s, Wang Mingdao. After the Chinese student movement closed down in the early 1950s he was imprisoned for close on forty years. He was nearly blind when he was released about four or five years ago, just before he died. A Christian from the West interviewed him – I have a copy of the tape. He put this question to him: 'After all the years that you have spent in solitary confinement, do you not feel any hint of bitterness towards God? How do you look now upon the years that you spent in isolation in prison?'

He said, 'I don't feel any sense of bitterness. For me, the time in solitary confinement was "a honeymoon with Jesus".' Sounds rather glib, doesn't it? Except that that really was his experience.

Richard Wurmbrand, another towering intellect – a Romanian pastor, very old now – served many years in solitary confinement. In his *Sermons in Solitary Confinement*, which he composed in prison and then wrote up afterwards, he said this: 'Often at night I danced for joy in my cell, because I was aware of the presence of God.' God made his presence known to those believers in the thickest of darkness, as the psalmist tells us.

Now, some of you may go through dark experiences in the future. You may be going through some now; you may be affected by the divorce of parents, you may be losing a parent who is sick or ill, or even a brother or sister; you may be going through some other problem.

I always find that verse in Isaiah a great comfort, where the prophet speaks of God's attitude to the believer: 'A bruised reed he will not break, and a smouldering wick he will not snuff out' (Is. 42:3). What is he implying? Well, some of us as believers are like bruised reeds, hanging to one side. The natural thing to do is to snap the top off and throw it away. God says that some of his children are dysfunctional, weakened like bruised reeds; but he will not break them off. He says, 'The smouldering wick I will not snuff out.' Some of you are like that. At Christmas time when we have candles, you can see smoke rising from a candle that has just been extinguished. The natural inclination is to pinch the wick and snuff the plume of smoke out. God says that some believers are like that. You may be like a smouldering wick. But, he says, 'I will not snuff you out.' Instead, he promises his presence to believers.

The second application: this passage teaches us that *the believer is never alone*. I always remember the story of Martin Goldsmith, a missionary in Singapore, taking his child to her school, which was situated at the top of a hill. At the bottom of the hill he said to her, 'You can walk up to school on your own now, can't you?'

She said, 'Yes, Daddy, of course, because Jesus is with me.'

And she walked up the hill holding her hand in the air as if Jesus was holding her hand. He thought that a beautiful picture of the presence of Christ.

It highlights the fact that for believers born after the New Testament era, we are indwelt by the Spirit of God and have the Spirit of Christ dwelling in us. In the Old Testament Noah knew six or seven believers, Abel hardly anyone; Joseph was alone in Egypt; Lot . . . Jeremiah . . . Rahab . . . no Bible, no church, no Word Alive, no Bible overviews, no Roy Clements, no Jonathan Lamb . . . . You have much, much more.

Yet they knew the presence of God. And if he could keep them, he can keep you no matter what your circumstances. The believer is never alone. Some people talk, if they are single, as if they are going to be alone through life. But God promises by his Spirit to accompany them, as Jonathan Lamb highlighted last night in his talk.

A third application is that this chapter teaches us that *this is a lifelong promise leading into eternity*. There is a delightful phrase in Philippians where Paul says to the Philippian church (who are afraid of being left on their own, as the great apostle is about to be taken out of their way), 'I have every confidence that God will bring to completion the work which he has begun in you' (*cf.* Phil. 1:6). Handley Moule, a wonderful commentator, translated this as 'I have every confidence that God by his presence will put the finishing touches to what he has begun in your life'.

The New Testament is replete with promises of the presence of God to the believer. 'I will never leave you, nor forsake you' (Heb. 13:5, AV); 'None shall pluck you from my hand' (*cf.* Jn. 10:28); 'Come near to God and he will come near to you' (Jas. 4:8). But one of the most powerful phrases is in the Old Testament, in 1 Samuel 12:22, where God says this: 'The LORD will not forsake his people' – why? – 'for his great name's sake' (AV). God cannot forsake the believer, for his own honour is at stake. So he'll stick with you through thick and thin.

And in the New Testament in the book of Colossians we have that wonderful verse that talks about Christ being in us, the hope of glory, and emphasizes the all-sufficiency of Christ, who dwells within us (Col. 1:27). It could read, 'If you have Christ you have *epignōsis*', which is a Greek technical name for the decisive knowledge of God – all that you need of God is dwelling in you in the glorious person of the Lord Jesus Christ by his Spirit.

So there were two things that held these three men together. Firstly, they understood that God was the sovereign Lord of the universe. Do you reflect on the promises and the references to the sovereignty of God in Scripture? Secondly, they knew God's presence, and we today know God's presence by his Spirit, the Spirit of Christ dwelling in us. We need no more. Everything we have is in the person of Christ who dwells within us.

But there is a third reason that they stood firm, refused to fear and remained faithful.

They were convinced that the God they worshipped was true

This is very important. Goethe, the great German writer, once said, 'Woe betide the man or woman who tries to work out his or her principles in a time of crisis.' You can't do it; you must do it now, before the crisis arrives. That's why

Matthew Henry, an old commentator on this passage, puts it, delightfully: 'They resolved rather to die in their integrity than to live in their iniquity.'

All this week we have been focusing on strengthening foundations in the Christian life, to emphasize the fact that the Christian gospel is a true message given to us. So on Saturday night we focused on justification, which makes you at peace with God. On Sunday night the focus was on the uniqueness of Christ and his all-sufficiency; he is all we need. On Monday we focused on God's heart for the world, then last night Jonathan focused on knowing God's plan. Similarly, through the morning surveys – the authority of Scripture, the completeness of Scripture, replete with promises for our encouragement, help and our growth.

It is very important to strengthen your roots, so that you are solid before you are faced by times of temptation and difficulty. I remember asking my wife, after our daughter died, 'How is it that you have managed to stay firm and not give up walking with the Lord?'

She had spent a year with Francis Schaeffer, who I believe was one of the three great Christian leaders of the twentieth century. Schaeffer emphasized Christian apologetics. He emphasized the truthfulness of Scripture, that the Christian message was true, that we don't have to have exhaustive knowledge to believe but that we have sufficient knowledge.

And she said to me, 'Lindsay, the reason I have stood faithful is that Schaeffer taught me that the Christian message is the only truth. There is no answer to the problem of suffering in Islam or in Hinduism. I don't see a complete answer now as to why our daughter has suffered and died, but I do know that there is the hope of resurrection, of glory, of being with Christ, and also being with her in heaven in due course. I have no hope of that in existentialism, or Hinduism, or Islam, or secularism, or materialism or anything else. Where else can I turn, but to the truth of the Christian message?'

Do you believe that?

Do you believe it's really true?

Namby-pamby Christianity won't help you. A Christian faith that focuses on emotions and feelings (not that they are unimportant) won't help you in a time of crisis. You need to be convinced that it is true.

Last Easter we visited the south of France. I went to the museum of the Huguenots, where there is a reminder of Madame Durand, a very great Huguenot woman. Many of the men were imprisoned in those days, so the women did the evangelistic work. She was imprisoned in the Tour de Constance. You can see it today in the Camargue in the South of France, and the word that she wrote on the stone on the tower where she was kept for over thirty years is still there today: *Résister* – resist the devil and he will flee from you.

Why did she write that? Because she was convinced it was true. And unless you believe it is true in the time of fire, the furnace of the opposition from the evil one who will try to force you to look a second time at the commitments you made last night, you will not stand.

You have to come to the conviction that it is true. In our age and generation a cult of mindlessness is on the increase. Some people say, 'Only believe – ignore the mind! Strike for the heart.' In Sunday School one little boy, in answer to the question 'What is faith?' replied, 'Oh, it's believing something you know isn't true.'

That's the consequence of the loss of emphasis on understanding and on truth. The strong emphasis in our generation on 'experience as king' has meant a loss of emphasis on truth. It has also led to a failure to attempt to answer people's questions.

In this passage, the three men said to Nebuchadnezzar, 'We don't need to answer you.' That doesn't mean that they weren't prepared to give answers. In the previous chapter they gave him full and complete answers. but now they see that he is in such a rage, there is no point in speaking to him. That doesn't mean that we are not to give a reasoned defence of our convictions. If you fail to defend the faith, many will drift away.

A woman I know in her late sixties is a very sad soul. Her

mother died when she was nine, and as a consequence she was crippled through life: brought up in a Catholic convent and turned away from any concept of the Christian faith, because she felt that God didn't love her. When she was in the Catholic school, being brought up by the nuns, she asked them one day, 'Why do you think God allowed my mother to suffer?'

And one of the nuns said, 'You mustn't ask any questions.'

The Bible never says that anywhere. The Bible says we are fully allowed to ask questions. But as I quoted to you earlier, Francis Schaeffer says, 'We don't have exhaustive answers, but we do have sufficient in order to believe.' If you don't seek to answer the questions, if you don't seek to build up your conviction that it is true, it will lead to a falling away of the faithful. It will lead to a separation of secular and sacred, and to faith being allowed to affect only limited areas of our lives.

It is very important to strengthen your roots, to strengthen your doctrinal convictions and your understanding. Some people feel that 'doctrine' is a dirty word. When I went to university, one of the deacons in my church said, 'Lindsay, doctrine is dry.' That's nonsense. In the Song of Moses in Deuteronomy God says this: 'Hear, O earth, the words of my mouth. Let my teaching [my doctrine, my truth] fall like rain and my words descend like dew' (Dt. 32:1–2). The purpose of Christian truth is to refresh, strengthen and renew the believer. That's the purpose of truth: to equip him or her to stand for the cause of the gospel. That's how these people stood. They really believed it was true; they had no doubt that the God they worshipped was the true God.

There is one final thing on which I want to comment.

Their confidence was held in tension with a jealous concern for God's glory

They must have known of the reference in Exodus 20, where God gives the Ten Commandments and prohibits worshipping and bowing down to false idols for the reason that he is a jealous God, jealous for his glory: he resents the presence of a rival.

And in a sense they shared this sense of jealousy for God's glory. They refused to share the worship with anyone else, which they were offering to him alone. This is one of the primary motivating factors for many people in Christian service: they are compelled by a jealous concern for God's glory. In the New Testament Paul put it another way: 'I glory in Christ' – thirty-six times he said it. It was the kind of motivation that drove many of the great missionaries of history.

One example is Henry Martyn, and with this I must close. Martyn was a brilliant Cambridge maths graduate in the last century. He was also a gifted linguist: he went to Persia, modern Iran, and began the translation of the Scriptures into several languages. He died at the age of twenty-nine, and never married. Some of his correspondence with his fiancée has been preserved, in which he writes, 'We cannot marry yet: my love must wait, because I have a task here to be completed.' The love was never consummated.

He wrote to her once of how a Muslim mullah came to him at a time when Iran and Russia were at war (the former was recognized as a Muslim country, the latter a Christian one). The mullah said, 'I had a dream last night, a vision: and in this dream your Jesus fell at the feet of my Muhammad and pleaded with him for mercy, to stop the slaughter of the Russian Christian soldiers.'

Martyn wrote, 'I was cut to the soul by this blasphemy. I could not endure existence if Jesus were not glorified. It would be hell for me if he were always thus dishonoured. I am wounded when Christ is insulted.'

That's the kind of image you get of Shadrach, Meshach and Abednego. They were wounded when the God they worshipped was insulted. Are you?

If you have no sense of jealousy for the glory of God, nothing will compel you through thick and thin to stand for him in the highways and byways of Britain or the ends of the earth. Pray and cry out to God, that, like Henry Martyn, and like Shadrach, Meshach and Abednego, you will have a jealousy for the glory of God.

So, dear brothers and sisters, I must come to a close. If you do not want to be gripped by fear in the Christian life but want to serve faithfully, whether at home or overseas, wherever God calls you, may I exhort you to remember these lessons from the story of Shadrach, Meshach and Abednego. They are strong slabs or foundations to build your life on. Trust God's sovereign purposes for your life. Secondly, remember he is near, and draw near to him day by day – Moses said to the Israelites, 'Consecrate yourselves day by day to the Lord' – not once or now and again, but day after day. Thirdly, solidify your convictions and your foundations, your roots in the Christian life, so you come to the absolute certainty that it is true, and worth defending before any man or woman, king or pauper. And fourthly, ask God to cultivate in your spirit a holy jealousy for his glory.

If this happens in your life you will become a potent weapon, usable by the Holy Spirit for God's glory.

Word Alive 1993 tapes

Copies are available for sale from:

ICC
Silverdale Rd
Eastbourne
East Sussex
BN20 7AB

Telephone: 0323 643341
Fax: 0323 649240